Top Careers in Two Years

Public Safety, Law, and Security

Titles in the *Top Careers in Two Years* Series

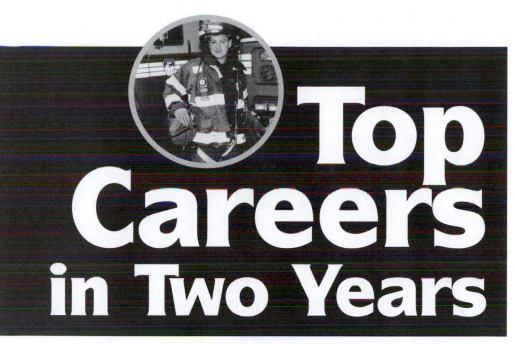

Top Careers in Two Years

Public Safety, Law, and Security

By Lisa Cornelio and Gail Eisenberg

Ferguson Publishing
An imprint of Infobase Publishing

Top Careers in Two Years

Public Safety, Law, and Security

Ferguson
An imprint of Infobase Publishing
132 West 31st Street
New York, NY 10001

ISBN-13: 978-0-8160-6904-0
ISBN-10: 0-8160-6904-2

Library of Congress Cataloging-in-Publication Data

Top careers in two years.
    v. cm.
  Includes index.
  Contents: v. 1. Food, agriculture, and natural resources / by Scott Gillam — v. 2. Construction and trades / Deborah Porterfield — v. 3. Communications and the arts / Claire Wyckoff — v. 4. Business, finance, and government administration / Celia W. Seupal — v. 5. Education and social services / Jessica Cohn — v. 6. Health care, medicine, and science / Deborah Porterfield — v. 7. Hospitality, human services, and tourism / Rowan Riley — v. 8. Computers and information technology / Claire Wyckoff — v. 9. Public safety, law, and security / Lisa Cornelio, Gail Eisenberg — v. 10. Manufacturing and transportation — v. 11. Retail, marketing, and sales / Paul Stinson.
  ISBN-13: 978-0-8160-6896-8 (v. 1 : hc : alk. paper)
  ISBN-10: 0-8160-6896-8 (v. 1 : hc : alk. paper)
  ISBN-13: 978-0-8160-6897-5 (v. 2 : hc. : alk. paper)
  ISBN-10: 0-8160-6897-6 (v. 2 : hc. : alk. paper)
  ISBN-13: 978-0-8160-6898-2 (v. 3 : hc : alk. paper)
  ISBN-10: 0-8160-6898-4 (v. 3 : hc : alk. paper)
  ISBN-13: 978-0-8160-6899-9 (v. 4 : hc : alk. paper)
  ISBN-10: 0-8160-6899-2 (v. 4 : hc : alk. paper)
  ISBN-13: 978-0-8160-6900-2 (v. 5 : hc : alk. paper)
  ISBN-10: 0-8160-6900-X (v. 5 : hc : alk. paper)
  ISBN-13: 978-0-8160-6901-9 (v. 6 : hc : alk. paper)
  ISBN-10: 0-8160-6901-8 (v. 6 : hc : alk. paper)
  ISBN-13: 978-0-8160-6902-6 (v. 7 : hc : alk. paper)
  ISBN-10: 0-8160-6902-6 (v. 7 : hc : alk. paper)
  ISBN-13: 978-0-8160-6903-3 (v. 8 : hc : alk. paper)
  ISBN-10: 0-8160-6903-4 (v. 8 : hc : alk. paper)
  ISBN-13: 978-0-8160-6904-0 (v. 9 : hc : alk. paper)
  ISBN-10: 0-8160-6904-2 (v. 9 : hc : alk. paper)
  ISBN-13: 978-0-8160-6905-7 (v. 10 : hc : alk. paper)
  ISBN-10: 0-8160-6905-0 (v. 10 : hc : alk. paper)
  ISBN-13: 978-0-8160-6906-4 (v. 11 : hc : alk. paper)
  ISBN-10: 0-8160-6906-9 (v. 11 : hc : alk. paper)
  1. Vocational guidance—United States. 2. Occupations—United States. 3. Professions—United States.
  HF5382.5.U5T677 2007
  331.7020973—dc22
                                                              2006028638

Ferguson books are available at special discounts when purchased in bulk quantities for businesses, associations, institutions, or sales promotions. Please call our Special Sales Department in New York at (212) 967-8800 or (800) 322-8755.

You can find Ferguson on the World Wide Web at http://www.fergpubco.com

Produced by Print Matters, Inc.
Text design by A Good Thing, Inc.
Cover design by Salvatore Luongo

Printed in the United States of America

Sheridan PMI 10 9 8 7 6 5 4 3 2 1

This book is printed on acid-free paper.

Contents

How to Use This Book

This book, part of the *Top Careers in Two Years* series, highlights in-demand careers for readers considering a two-year degree program—either straight out of high school or after working a job that does not require advanced education. The focus throughout is on the fastest-growing jobs with the best potential for advancement in the field. Readers learn about future prospects while discovering jobs they may never have heard of.

An associate's degree can be a powerful tool in launching a career. This book tells you how to use it to your advantage, explore job opportunities, and find local degree programs that meet your needs.

Each chapter provides the essential information needed to find not just a job but a career that fits your particular skills and interests. All chapters include the following features:

- "Vital Statistics" provides crucial information at a glance, such as salary range, employment prospects, education or training needed, and work environment.

- Discussion of salary and wages notes hourly versus salaried situations as well as potential benefits. Salary ranges take into account regional differences across the United States.

- "Keys to Success" is a checklist of personal skills and interests needed to thrive in the career.

- "A Typical Day at Work" describes what to expect at a typical day on the job.

- "Two-Year Training" lays out the value of an associate's degree for that career and what you can expect to learn.

- "What to Look For in a School" provides questions to ask and factors to keep in mind when selecting a two-year program.

- "The Future" discusses prospects for the career going forward.

- "Interview with a Professional" presents firsthand information from someone working in the field.

- ⚷ "Job Seeking Tips" offers suggestions on how to meet and work with people in the field, including how to get an internship or apprenticeship.

- ⚷ "Career Connections" lists Web addresses of trade organizations providing more information about the career.

- ⚷ "Associate's Degree Programs" provides a sampling of some of the better-known two-year schools.

- ⚷ "Financial Aid" provides career-specific resources for financial aid.

- ⚷ "Related Careers" lists similar related careers to consider.

In addition to a handy comprehensive index, the back of the book features two appendices providing invaluable information on job hunting and financial aid. Appendix A, Tools for Career Success, provides general tips on interviewing either for a job or two-year program, constructing a strong résumé, and gathering professional references. Appendix B, Financial Aid, introduces the process of applying for aid and includes information about potential sources of aid, who qualifies, how to prepare an application, and much more.

Introduction

As you begin to think about life after high school, you will contemplate whether to continue your education. If the thought of a four-year degree seems a little intimidating, here's some good news. Associate's degrees, which can be completed in two years or less, offer a great alternative to four-year degrees in many ways. First, they are much more affordable than most private four-year colleges. Tuition and fees for a two-year program average $2,191 a year, while tuition at a four-year private college costs an average of $21,235 a year, according to the College Board. With a two-year program, chances are you can also avoid expensive room and board fees by living nearby while you work on your degree. That's because most communities have two-year schools in convenient locations. What's more, the cost of an associate's degree is increasing more slowly than that of a bachelor's degree, with financial aid for those attending trade, technical, vocational, two-year, and career colleges just as plentiful as it is for four-year colleges. Grant aid for two-year degrees averages $2,300 per student. This aid is often supplemented by employers, who may be happy to increase the proficiency of their staffs by providing loans, scholarships, and flexible schedules so that their employees can achieve associate's degrees.

Indeed, flexibility is a primary reason many students enroll in two-year programs. Night and weekend classes are reasonable options for many working students, and the expanding world of online degrees ensures that no matter where you live or what kind of schedule you have, a two-year degree is within your reach. Two-year degrees are also more accessible to those who may not have performed well in high school; admission to most programs is not overly competitive, unlike admission to four-year colleges, which often hinges on test scores and high grade point averages.

Another appealing aspect of two-year degrees includes the hands-on experience that so many associate's programs provide. This experience often leads to greater levels of responsibility on the job, because employers are more likely to trust and value new employees who have already worked in the field. Employers also appreciate the commitment and focus that degree holders have shown, which can lead to positions of both increased responsibility and higher earnings.

Schools with strong public safety, law, and security programs, in particular, encourage their students to seek out internships and volunteer positions while they work toward their degrees. Such experience is a highly valuable addition to any résumé, particularly in this quickly expanding field. Many seasoned law enforcement workers, ex-military personnel, and recent retirees from the field may be among your competition, so practical experience will provide the lift that many entry-level job hunters require.

Associate's degree holders earn more than high school grads ($2,000–$6,000 a year more on average) and also face a much lower rate of unemployment. Two-year grads often parlay this good fortune into a four-year degree, transferring credits from their associate's program to a four-year college. Many times their employers pick up all or part of the tab on additional training, especially in public safety, law, and security professions, which depend on continued education to familiarize workers with new technology and challenges in their fields. Further, according to the Bureau of Labor Statistics, there is greater growth in occupations requiring associate's degrees than in occupations requiring other types of training. Clearly, associate's degrees offer a great way to get your foot in the door quickly, conveniently, and inexpensively.

Careers in Public Safety, Law, and Security

So you're sold on a two-year degree. Now the question may be what job area. Within this volume, *Public Safety, Law, and Security*, are the careers that focus on protecting the public, preventing crimes, and responding to emergencies. In particular, these jobs include law enforcement, legal work, and private and homeland security. Today these positions are more important than ever as the country faces new and unpredictable threats and challenges. Rolling blackouts from three-digit heat waves, the challenge of protecting vulnerable ports and transit systems, and threats of biochemical warfare are all part of the twenty-first century landscape. First responders—fire, police, and emergency medical personnel—are on the front lines of this new world. Eighty percent of them have been educated at community colleges.

What's more, the role of first responders now extends well beyond the duties of the past. In addition to the 200 million 9-1-1 calls received each year, emergency workers must now be prepared for unique and unexpected challenges such as bio-terrorism and dirty bombs. These professionals are part of the homeland security force that is as varied as the threats themselves. As Ellen Gordon, a member of the Senior Advisory Council for the Department of Homeland Security, says, "I see within the next 20 to 25 years that the community colleges are going to be the base for training and education for all the different areas within our homeland security."

Although the public often assumes that major cities are the only targets of attack, every state in the nation and every province in Canada remains vulnerable. Water supplies and rivers, crops and cattle, railways and highways are all at risk in this new age. As concerns about safety increase, the public needs to be assured that their communities have the proper resources and staff that a changing world demands. Yet police, fire, and emergency medical forces are expected to lose large portions of their workforce to early retirement and private sector opportunities, and this workforce will need to be replenished. A two-year degree is the first step to becoming a skilled and respected worker on the forefront of the battle to protect against threats and emergencies of every kind.

The jobs held by first responders are not the only ones highlighted in this volume. Other positions involve responsibilities that range from the protection of our natural resources to the supervision of criminals and managing a crime scene. Each of these careers plays an important role in the safety of every community. "There are a lot of great opportunities in criminal justice for people with all types of interests," stresses John Landry, a criminal justice coordinator at Keiser College in West Palm Beach, Florida. "We are not just about cops driving around." For instance, park rangers guard and protect federal, state, and local parks and historic landmarks. They also enforce laws that ensure that these natural resources and recreation areas are preserved for coming generations. Crime scene technicians and private security specialists do their best to prevent crimes and help catch and convict the criminals who commit them. Finally, paralegals and legal secretaries help the justice system run smoothly and fairly, assisting lawyers and judges so that cases are managed properly, laws are followed, and lawbreakers receive appropriate penalties. The good news is that all of these professions are vital and are growing—the U.S. Department of Labor, for instance, predicts a 29 percent increase in criminal justice–related positions by 2010.

Choosing a Career in Public Safety, Law, and Security

As you try to pick from among the wide variety of public safety, law, and security jobs, it's a good idea to ask yourself some questions. Are you interested in a number of fields, but hoping to gain experience before you commit to one area? Do you like having the same routine every day or is variety important to you? Are you comfortable being visible in positions of authority or would you rather work behind the scenes? Understanding your own personal preferences will help to ensure that you make wise decisions when it comes to choosing your career.

For instance, it helps to understand that many positions in public safety, law, and security share certain elements. A number of jobs in these fields require that you wear a uniform. Even positions that permit civilian clothes to be worn require that they be clean, neat, and fairly traditional. If you work in public safety, law, and security, the people you serve must be able to trust you and your judgment. Your personal appearance is the first indication of how reliable you are.

Another important criterion for choosing among public safety, law, and security jobs is whether you're willing and able to carry a firearm. Some jobs in this field require that you do this. You must be ready to use the firearm if a situation arises that requires the use of force. This is not a responsibility to be taken lightly, so make sure you really think about this possibility before you commit to a career that may require the use of force.

Many of the positions discussed in this volume also require an ability to confront those who are breaking the law or violating rules. This is not always an easy task, but if it's part of your job, you need to enforce laws and take the appropriate measures when people break them.

First responder positions may appeal to you if you are good in a crisis. You may confront some of the most difficult sights and situations imaginable, from violent crime scenes to terrible car accidents. Victims may be near death, in deep trauma, or the witnesses of deeply disturbing scenes. Fortunately, you will also see people at their best and most heroic, as well. Regardless, as a professional, you must remain cool and calm and do your job, despite the pressure, danger, and chaos around you.

Other elements that many security and law-related jobs share are shift work, unpredictable hours, and overtime. If you choose a career in one of these fields, you may not be able to depend on getting New Year's Eve off or making it to your best friend's bachelor party. Maybe you'll stay up for 24 hours straight as you work with your peers to fight a fire, prepare for a hurricane, or investigate a crime scene. Perhaps you'll be called out in the middle of the night to respond to incidents of domestic violence. You must be prepared for such scenarios if you are considering a career in public safety, law, or security.

Despite the dangers, inconveniences, and often tough working conditions, without a doubt, jobs in public safety, law, and security can lead to great career satisfaction and a lasting sense of reward. Of course, some of the jobs discussed in this volume are more conventional, with steady hours and predictable workdays. However, as many who work in these fields will tell you, one of the best things about these careers is that no two days are the same. Every shift presents a new challenge, a chance to learn, and most importantly, the opportunity to help others.

Helping others is often the number one reason why people enter careers in public safety, law, and security. To do that, they must be team players, working together to solve crimes, tend to those in need, and enforce laws. Whether it's protection of a neighborhood, an entire town, a state park, or even the nation at large, people in public safety, law, and security provide an essential service. That provides a sense of reward every time they go to work. In addition, careers in these fields come with great benefits, excellent job stability, and enormous respect from the community. Despite days that may be incredibly frustrating and disappointing, job satisfaction is higher than average in these fields.

Preparing for a Career in Public Safety, Law, and Security

So, how do you prepare for a future in public safety, law, and security? Each chapter outlines different steps to take to make yourself a more appealing candidate. For example, a résumé that shows that you are responsible is an important element in applying for a position in public safety, law, and security. Internships and part-time jobs help prove that you are dependable and trustworthy. Volunteer work is another way to strengthen your résumé: More than 60 percent of hiring managers say they count volunteer work as relevant experience (according to careerbuilder.com). These positions also can serve as resources for references and contacts as you begin your job search; so always put your best foot forward during summer jobs and other extracurricular activities.

Keep in mind that employers are becoming savvier in their hiring processes. This is nowhere more apparent—or more important—than in public safety, law, and security, where paper trails are examined closely. Many positions require extensive background checks and sometimes security clearances. Felonies and misdemeanors often disqualify applicants from certain jobs, as do poor credit histories and spotty driving records. In the age of the Internet, Google, and Web sites like Myspace.com, employers are able to uncover unappealing personal information such as how many beers you can drink or your favorite curse words. Be as impeccable with your public persona as you are with your personal appearance, and no red flags will be raised when you apply for a job. Remember, you will be seen as a role model in this field, so keep that in mind as you finish high school.

Finally, as you begin to think about your future, do whatever you can to learn more about the fields that interest you. Reading this book is a good first step; follow through on the many other resources it suggests, such as researching various jobs online, talking to professionals in the field, and volunteering with local organizations that do work related to your interests. The more you know, the better prepared you will be to tackle the very competitive but rewarding job market of public safety, law, and security.

Firefighter

Vital Statistics

Salary: The median yearly income is about $38,000, according to 2006 data from the U.S. Bureau of Labor Statistics.

Employment: Competition is high; however, this field is expected to grow faster than the average for all occupations through 2014, according to the Bureau of Labor Statistics.

Education: An associate's degree in fire technology can aid an applicant's chances in this competitive field. Candidates must also pass written, physical, and background exams and be at least 18 years old.

Work Environment: While firefighters spend a great deal of time at the station, when they respond to calls they work in dangerous conditions indoors and outdoors.

September 11 put firefighters in the public eye in a way no American has seen before. The heroes we all witnessed that day inspired many to seek their futures in firefighting. As a result, competition to become a firefighter has increased. Fortunately, there is also a greater need for qualified firefighters, partially because of the increased risk of threats we now face. These threats have resulted in growing public concern that every community be as prepared as possible in the event of an emergency. Such preparation has brought more attention to building evacuation plans and managing the public when a crisis occurs. Natural disasters such as Hurricane Katrina and the rampant wildfires out West have also elevated the profile of firefighters in the past few years, ensuring that even with budget cuts, firefighters' positions will be maintained.

These positions are vital in our communities because firefighters are usually the first to respond to car accidents, hazardous-waste spills, plane crashes, bomb threats, elevator rescues, floods, and water and ice rescues. They often work in tandem with emergency medical technicians (EMTs) and are trained to provide much of the same pre-hospital medical care that EMTs offer. Firefighters enter endangered structures, provide ventilation, and search for possible victims. They then rescue those victims by removing them from the scene and using lifesaving techniques such as cardiopulmonary resuscitation (CPR), if necessary. Firefighters are also responsible for salvaging property and securing damaged sites. Finally, firefighters provide education to the public about fire safety, and they inspect buildings for code violations and the proper installation of sprinkler systems and other protective devices.

All firefighters are members of a team that they live and work with at the station. This team becomes a surrogate family, and more and more this family includes women: Recent statistics show that nearly a quarter of a million firefighters are female. In fact, as of April 2006, there were at least 31 career-level or combination (i.e., with some career and some volunteer personnel) U.S. fire agencies whose top-level chief was a woman. However, the road is often tough for these female firefighters as they may face resistance from their male peers.

Yet everyone from rookies to captains does his or her share to take care of one another, the station, and the community they serve. While each person in the department has a special task, they all come together to provide an essential service that is never taken for granted. If you're thinking of joining such a hard-working and dedicated team, you must be sure of being able to work long hours in close proximity with fellow firefighters and being willing to put your life on the line to protect and serve others.

On the Job

The image of firefighters in the movies is one of danger and excitement, filled with life-threatening situations and narrow escapes. While such scenes can be part of firefighters' experience, they have many other responsibilities as well. The firefighters on duty must evaluate incoming calls and react accordingly; a minor kitchen fire demands a very different response from a major industrial blaze. Firefighters must drive the appropriate vehicles to the scene, choose the best route, and arrive safely and quickly. Once on scene, excellent communication skills and ability to follow orders are essential.

Firefighters must be incredibly fit: The clothing and equipment they wear can weigh between 30 and 100 pounds. In addition, the machinery they operate requires great strength and dexterity. Tools such as circular saws, breathing apparatuses, and the famous "jaws of life," used to free victims from steel and concrete structures, can mean the difference between life and death and must be operated correctly at all times. There is very little room for error in emergency situations, so every firefighter must be level-headed and able to make quick and intelligent decisions. While still maintaining their optimism and willingness to be of service, firefighters also must deal with the loss of life and pain that disaster may cause.

Firefighting can take place in the expansive forests of our national parks or in the narrow, dark hallways of a burning building. Firefighters are exposed to many dangers, from leaping flames to toxic smoke to falling debris. Shifts, which vary but may last for 24 hours, can pass with no calls or be filled with a five-alarm blaze that is fought for days. Very few professions can offer the variety and excitement that firefighters enjoy, but it is also not a career for the faint of heart.

🔑 Keys to Success

To be a successful firefighter, you should have

- 🗝 physical stamina
- 🗝 excellent communication skills
- 🗝 the ability to follow orders
- 🗝 stress management skills
- 🗝 common sense
- 🗝 decision-making abilities

Do You Have What It Takes?

Students interested in becoming firefighters should be physically fit, able to handle stress, and motivated to help others. Manual dexterity, decisiveness, and the desire to be part of a team are high on the list of requirements for all firefighters. Competition to become a firefighter is tough, so you must be prepared to endure long training periods as well as written exams and interviews. Also you must pass medical, psychological, and background tests both as a candidate as well as annually for as long as you serve. A clean driving record, and CPR and EMT certification are often required. Perhaps most important, you must be willing to put your life in danger to save others.

A Typical Day at Work

Shifts at most firehouses often last for 24 hours, which means that in addition to fighting fires, you eat, sleep, and maintain the station as part of your normal routine. If there is a call during your shift, you may be responsible for driving the truck or other emergency vehicle; operating hoses, pumps, and ladders; gaining entry to the scene; and providing ventilation. You may be involved in search and rescue duties and emergency medical care, as well.

Back at the station, you are expected to maintain all vehicles and equipment, making sure that everything is clean and in good working order and notifying others when repairs are needed. The station itself must be kept tidy as well, and each department's firefighters do all of their food shopping and cooking.

Finally, as a firefighter, you often inspect buildings for safety devices and code violations and provide the public with information, both at the scene of emergencies and as part of the larger community. You are also expected to continue to keep informed of developments in firefighting techniques and attend routine training sessions.

How to Break In

Determining which fire departments are hiring may take some research. Begin with the print and online want ads of your local paper, especially the Sunday edition, but check major cities' newspapers as well. The Internet is another source you should investigate. Web sites such as http://www .firehouse.com and http://www.firecareers.com require subscriptions, but they are well worth it. Publications such as *Firehouse* magazine occasionally list opportunities as well. City or county human resource and personnel offices often handle the testing for fire departments, so be sure to call for testing information as well as openings. Always follow up on leads from these offices with the fire departments themselves to confirm your information. Local volunteer programs can provide you with hiring information, as can bulletin boards at colleges that offer EMT and paramedic programs. Since the testing includes a physical component, you may want to start training well in advance of the test date.

> ## "All men are created equal, then a few become firemen."
> —Author unknown

Two-Year Training

A two-year associate's degree in fire science technology not only makes you a more appealing candidate in a very competitive field, but it also sets you on track for continued success and advancement. Classes in fire technology range from the fundamentals of hazardous materials to building construction and reading blueprints to fire prevention and safety. Some schools concentrate on classroom learning, while others combine academics with hands-on experience.

Remember, a two-year degree in fire technology does not guarantee you a spot on your local squad. You must also pass the appropriate medical, physical, and background tests before you will be considered as an applicant. Some fire departments have volunteer programs, which are great ways to strengthen your training and become a better candidate.

Before you can become an active-duty firefighter, you must spend about 600 hours in training over the course of several months. This instruction often occurs in the department's training center or academy, where you learn firefighting techniques, fire prevention, hazardous materials control, local building codes, first aid, and CPR. You are introduced to the tools of firefighting, such as axes, chain saws, fire extinguishers, ladders, and other specialized equipment as well. If you complete the training successfully, you are assigned to a department and begin your probationary year, a period in which your skills will be constantly tested and evaluated.

Your training does not stop after you become a permanent staff member. Firefighters are expected to participate in professional development through training drills and classes. A four-year degree often is required to advance to the rank of lieutenant or captain. You can also pursue related careers such as fire investigator and prevention specialist.

What to Look For in a School

When considering a two-year school, be sure to ask these questions:

☞ Will the course prepare me to pass the written exams of fire departments in my area and beyond?

☞ What kind of relationship does the program have with area fire departments? Are internships with area departments available through the school?

☞ What are the professors' credentials? Are any of the instructors either working firefighters or retired from fire service?

☞ Does the school offer career guidance and provide contacts for seeking positions both in your area and beyond?

The Future

The National Fire Protection Association (NFPA) estimates that there were more than 1.1 million firefighters in the United States in 2004. Of those, 27 percent were professional and 73 percent were volunteer. Most of the paid firefighters were in communities with more than 25,000 people. Today, the number of career firefighters is up, with 2004 showing the highest number of career firefighters ever recorded, while the number of volunteers is decreasing slightly. Yet since most firefighters love their jobs, they tend to stay in their positions for 20 to 40 years. As a result, competition for jobs is high. However, the growth and development of communities often increase the need for firefighters. Two other important factors are affecting opportunities in firefighting. First, many firefighters who joined departments during hiring drives in the 1970s now qualify for retirement. Some experts estimate that as much as 50 percent of the nation's firefighting force will be replaced in the coming years. Post-9/11 concerns also have increased the awareness of the critical role fire departments play in national security. The Bureau of Labor Statistics estimates that there will be a 24 percent increase in the number of professional firefighters in the next seven years. More and more, firefighting is transforming from a vocation to a profession. As such, associate's degrees are becoming the norm rather than the exception with new hires; almost 58 percent of firefighters between the ages of 25 and 44 have some college education.

Interview with a Professional:
Q&A
Brian Flynn
Firefighter, 39 Engine, 16 Truck, FDNY,
New York, New York

Q: *How did you get started?*

A: After 9/11 I realized I wanted to do something that could help people; I wanted a profession that was a job of honor. I knew being a firefighter would fulfill this goal.

Q: *What's a typical day like?*

A: There are two tours of duty. A day tour begins with breakfast and is followed by committee work. All firefighters participate in this activity, which includes cleaning the kitchen, apparatus floor, officers' rooms, rigs, bunk room, and bathrooms. Following committee work there might be building inspection duties, or BI. Then there's Drill, where an officer picks a topic, tool, procedure, just about anything fire-related. All members discuss it and, in the process, many times retrain on the topic. Of course, all action stops if there's an emergency and attention is directed to the call.

Q: *What's your advice for those starting a career?*

A: Take a class or purchase a study guide to prepare [for the firefighter's exam] and take it seriously. The higher you score, the earlier you'll be called for the physical. If you have the time to take more classes, by all means do so. Stay in shape . . . run, weight lift, and stretch regularly. Firefighting is a very physically demanding job. Have a positive outlook and be motivated throughout the process and your whole career.

Q: *What's the best part of being a firefighter?*

A: Being trained to help people brings a tremendous feeling of satisfaction, accomplishment, and self-worth. If you're fortunate enough to save a life as a firefighter, it's the ultimate reward. The brotherhood or sisterhood of firefighters is very real and makes this job different from many others. We live as a family—eat, sleep, and work together. We protect and look out for each other. It's a dangerous occupation, but the best one in the world.

Did You Know?

Every 20 seconds a fire department responds to a fire somewhere in the nation.

Job Seeking Tips

See the suggestions below and turn to Appendix A for advice on résumés and interviews.

- ✔ Learn as much as you can about the department to which you'll be applying. Requirements such as driver's license and EMT and CPR certification vary, although those qualifications will only help you.
- ✔ Get in top physical condition.
- ✔ Maintain a clean driving record.
- ✔ Volunteer with your local department, if possible.
- ✔ Network with local firefighters and other friends seeking positions in fire services.
- ✔ Surf the Internet for training tips and advice from real firefighters.

Career Connections

For more information on a career in firefighting, look up these sources of information.

A few of the country's top fire departments http://www.fireprep.com/top_150_fire_departments.html

Association of Fire Fighters http://www.iaff.org

U.S. Fire Administration http://www.usfa.dhs.gov

The National Fire Academy http://www.usfa.dhs.gov/training/nfa

Ontario Fire Marshal http://www.ofm.gov.on.ca

Associate's Degree Programs

Here are a few schools with two-year firefighting programs:

Santa Ana Community College, Santa Ana, California

Red Rocks Community College, Lakewood, Colorado

Northern Virginia Community College, Annandale, Virginia

John Wood Community College, Quincy, Illinois, also offers online degrees   http://www.jwcc.edu/instruct/fire

University of Cincinnati, Cincinnati, Ohio, also offers online degrees http://www.uc.edu

Financial Aid

For general information on financial aid for two-year students, see Appendix B.

The **National Fire Protection Association** lists several scholarships. http://www.nfpa.org

Related Careers

Forest fire inspector and prevention specialist, smoke jumper, fire inspector, fire investigator, fire protection specialist, and public fire educator.

Legal Secretary

Vital Statistics

Salary: The average annual salary for legal secretaries is $36,720, according to 2006 data from the U.S. Bureau of Labor and Statistics.

Employment: Employment of legal secretaries is projected to grow as fast as the average for all occupations through 2014, according to the Bureau of Labor and Statistics.

Education: An associate's degree with a major in "legal secretary" or paralegal studies provides instruction in keyboarding skills, word processing, and computer software and basic legal terminology, processes, and documents.

Work Environment: Most legal secretaries work in clean, comfortable offices, and occasionally in courts or law libraries.

The days of secretaries who simply pour their bosses coffee and make sure they aren't late for meetings are long gone. Today's ranks are filled with highly skilled professionals whose abilities range from computer software know-how to Internet research expertise. Legal secretaries are among the most esteemed of all, for not only do they have superior office skills, but they also have specialized legal knowledge. As a result, secretaries who work in law offices are often at the top of the pay scale when compared with secretaries in other fields.

Not to be confused with paralegals, who perform work that requires extensive knowledge of the law, legal secretaries assist lawyers by performing basic office duties as well as more specialized tasks related to the profession. As today's law offices become more technologically advanced, the responsibilities of legal secretaries are increasing. Personal and networked computers run word processing, desktop publishing, and legal software that must be supervised and managed by legal secretaries. Also contributing to the increased responsibilities of legal secretaries is the speed at which work is completed in today's modern law offices.

A career as a legal secretary requires a strong foundation in basic secretarial skills, such as keyboarding, dictation, and database management. Familiarity with fax machines, photocopiers, scanners, and complex telephone systems is also essential. However, increasingly today's legal secretaries provide support in areas that were once the domain of highly specialized computer technicians or even paralegals. Most attorneys are now able to manage many aspects of office work that would formerly have fallen on their secretaries, such as e-mail correspondence. As a result, legal secretaries are able to do more in less time as they juggle a wider range of tasks.

Their new responsibilities include Internet research and the preparation of legal documents such as subpoenas and summonses, contracts, and trial materials. Although many of these functions still require the supervision of an attorney, it is sophisticated work that calls for excellent written and communication skills as well as the ability to work efficiently and carefully.

While most legal secretaries are employed by large firms in major cities, employment also exists in small towns with lawyers in private practice. In fact, legal secretaries who work in smaller offices often have to be even more versatile to handle the wide variety of tasks. Firms with fewer attorneys must be able to handle everything from divorce hearings to bankruptcies, and legal secretaries must be familiar with the corresponding paperwork and procedures for each new assignment. Conversely, those who work in large firms may decide, after a few years on the job, to specialize in one area, such as real estate or litigation. Others may seek out work in the court system or in banks, insurance companies, government offices, and corporations that have in-house legal teams.

Regardless of the size of their office, legal secretaries are relied on to provide the liaison between the attorneys they work with and clients, the court system, and other firms. As such, they must have impeccable interpersonal skills and always be patient and discreet.

On the Job

Every day holds a new challenge in a law office, and legal secretaries must be flexible and skilled in many areas. You'll provide support for just one attorney or many and must be able to handle the pressing demands that legal work entails. Often, you'll be in the middle of one task, such as responding to a client's e-mail, when you'll be faced with another, more urgent request. Learning how to prioritize while remaining efficient and organized will be one of your biggest challenges.

Secretarial work is people oriented, so no matter how busy you get or how many people request your help, you must always remain courteous and patient to both clients and the attorneys for whom you work. Legal support staff must also maintain strict confidentiality of all details and aspects of clients' files and be sure to treat everyone with equal respect.

Most of your work will take place at your desk as you answer phones, respond to e-mail and other correspondence, and manage spreadsheets and presentation programs, such as the Microsoft Office Suite application PowerPoint on your computer. You should have a good grasp of the Internet and various services, such as LexisNexis, an Internet research system, and Westlaw, a legal research site. You may also be responsible for scheduling conferences and depositions—testimonies under oath—as well as handling travel arrangements. Both client billing and office payroll responsibilities may fall under your job description.

In addition to the secretarial support you will provide, you will be asked to proofread various legal documents and briefs and occasionally assist in other ways with legal research, perhaps by verifying quotes or locating resources. Legal secretaries typically work 40-hour weeks from 9 to 5, but during particularly busy times, you may be asked to work late or take work home with you. You can expect to be compensated for this extra effort with overtime pay and/or bonuses.

> **"No lawyer is so great that he or she doesn't make mistakes, and a good secretary can really save your behind on many of those occasions."**
> —Hans Sachs, a German public prosecutor

Keys to Success

To be a successful legal secretary, you should have

- excellent written and oral communication skills
- the ability to do multiple tasks at once
- good interpersonal skills
- a detail-oriented approach to your work
- a grasp of broad legal concepts
- strong organizational skills
- excellent judgment in making many critical decisions
- discretion regarding sensitive information

Do You Have What It Takes?

Students interested in a career as a legal secretary should excel at and enjoy courses involving research and writing. Proofreading skills are very important in legal secretarial work, so you should pay attention to detail and be able to edit your papers for grammar and spelling mistakes. While in high school, you should develop your keyboarding skills since most legal secretaries are required to type a minimum of 60 words per minute. You should also become familiar with Microsoft Office Suite software programs such as Excel. Summer work in an office will also make you a more attractive candidate and provide you with on-the-job experience.

A Typical Day at Work

The duties and tasks of legal secretaries vary widely, depending on the size and specialization of the firm. As a result, legal secretaries must be versatile and able to manage several tasks at once, from typing letters to requisitioning supplies. Lawyers rely on their legal secretaries to keep them well-informed and organized, so you must always be aware of schedules and office developments so that you can better assist them.

Entry-level legal secretaries are often given basic secretarial work such as filing and data entry until they become more familiar with legal office procedure and tasks. Your day may begin with answering calls from clients or sorting mail. Perhaps you will be placed on a special project in which you have to assemble files for a divorce case or proofread materials for a child custody battle. Very often, your assignment will have a deadline, and you will need to juggle your usual tasks in addition to the more time-sensitive ones to get everything done. Attorneys will rely on you to prioritize their requests over all your other responsibilities, so make sure you are comfortable handling many tasks at once.

How to Break In

While working on an associate's degree, aspiring legal secretaries can work in legal offices as mail clerks, data entry assistants, and receptionists. Not only does this provide an opportunity to develop basic office skills, but it also introduces you to the staff at large and lays the foundation for a future position. Two-year schools often offer internships at law firms or in the courts where valuable hands-on experience will help you become a more desirable job applicant when you finish your degree. As a high school student, see if any firms in your area hire students for summer employment. Courses in government, English composition, and business also can prepare you for a career as a legal secretary.

Two-Year Training

Two-year training for legal secretaries often falls under the "Applied Science" category in program listings. As a result, general education courses are part of the requirement. Classes in communications, composition, and mathematics complement more specialized courses, such as legal office procedures, legal transcription and research, and legal document production. Students gain specific administrative skills and background in legal terminology and processes. A strong emphasis is also placed on acquiring office skills such as keyboarding, word processing, and database management.

Typically, classroom work is often supplemented with internships or summer employment. Even after you earn your degree and complete an internship, there will be a training period wherever you work. To further boost your résumé, NALS (the National Association for Legal Professionals) offers two levels of credentials—the ALS (accredited legal secretary) and PLS (professional legal secretary). These optional certifications reflect your preparedness and commitment to your profession. They may also help you land a higher-paying position in a firm that specializes in a legal field that interests you, such as real estate or entertainment. If you do become drawn to a more specific area of the law, Legal Secretaries International offers a Certified Legal Secretary Specialist exam in six categories: business, litigation, criminal law, intellectual property, probate, and real estate.

What to Look For in a School

When considering a two-year school, be sure to ask these questions:

☞ Will this degree program provide both course work and the connections to an internship?

☞ What is the school's job placement rate?

☞ What are the professors' credentials? Have they worked in the profession? How available are the professors outside the classroom?

☞ What is the school's relationship with the local law community?

☞ Does the school provide training in the most current office technology?

The Future

Opportunities for legal secretaries will continue to expand as we increasingly rely on legal services in business, medicine, and our personal lives. Specialized fields such as malpractice law and intellectual property law are growing quickly. Litigation will offer many opportunities for legal secretaries. Improvements in technology have shifted the responsibilities of legal secretaries. More and more, they are relied on to keep pace with changing software and computer systems, often training their superiors in new programs. More than half of all legal secretaries have only high school degrees, so those with two-year degrees will have improved chances of finding positions with the potential to advance. The field as a whole is expected to grow by more than 17 percent by 2014, and men are increasingly joining the ranks of legal secretaries. If you are able to make yourself an indispensable member of your firm, your hard work could pay off, and you may be promoted to office manager. This would put you in charge of your firm's secretarial staff and possibly their paralegals.

Interview with a Professional:
Q&A

Joy Bridle
Legal secretary, Bereskin & Parr, Toronto,
Ontario, Canada

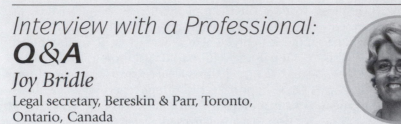

Q: *How did you get started?*

A: I had always found books related to lawyers, police, and crime intriguing, so when it came time to turn my attention to career choices, I signed up for a two-year Legal Secretarial course at Seneca College. My first position was with a large law firm, and I was able to dip my hand into each area of law. I found that intellectual property law dealt with a variety of issues each day, which kept things interesting.

Q: *What's a typical day like?*

A: Every day is challenging and rewarding. Whether I'm dealing with patents, trademarks, agreements, or licenses, time passes quickly, and I must prioritize the items that I wish to complete. Organizing and completing due dates in a timely fashion is my top priority. However, there are always a few curves thrown my way to keep things exciting. My boss relies on me to keep his practice running smoothly and trusts that I will make his workload lighter by taking care of as many issues as possible.

Q: *What's your advice for those starting a career?*

A: Knowledge is the key. Absorb as much as possible and ask a lot of questions. Personally, I like to know why things are done and the history behind the file, which assists me in understanding the issues at hand.

Q: *What's the best part of being a legal secretary?*

A: My favorite part is the interaction between me and my immediate boss, and me and the clients. I also enjoy helping everybody complete the necessary tasks in a timely fashion. Being connected to the clients, and assisting as much as possible provides a personal touch that I highly enjoy.

Did You Know?

Ruth Bader Ginsburg, appointed by former President Clinton to be the second female U.S. Supreme Court justice in history, worked as a legal secretary after getting her degree from Columbia Law School because law firms were not hiring women associates.

Job Seeking Tips

See the suggestions below and turn to Appendix A for advice on résumés and interviews.

✔ Decide what you're interested in and seek relevant experience.

✔ Talk to the career placement office at your school.

✔ If one area of the law appeals to you, such as real estate or bankruptcy, learn as much as you can about that field by taking relevant classes or seminars.

✔ Make sure your office skills, such as typing and dictation, are highly developed.

Career Connections

For more information on a career as a legal secretary, look up these sources of information.

Legal Secretaries International, Inc. http://www.legalsecretaries.org

The National Association for Legal Professionals http://www.nals.org

Legal Secretary Careers http://www.legalsecretarycareers.com

Associate's Degree Programs

Here are a few schools offering quality legal secretary programs:

Moraine Park Technical College, Beaver Dam, Fond du Lac, and West Bend, Wisconsin

Ridgewater College, Willmar, Minnesota

Renton Technical College, Renton, Washington

Seneca College, Toronto, Canada

Financial Aid

For general information on financial aid for two-year students, turn to Appendix B.

Legal Secretaries Incorporated provides the Eula Mae Jett Scholarship Plan to residents of California. http://www.lsi.org

Related Careers

Government secretary, legal receptionist, clerk, litigation practice assistant, legal word processor, and court reporter.

Paralegal

Vital Statistics

Salary: The yearly average salary for full-time paralegals is about $39,000, according to 2006 data from the U.S. Bureau of Labor Statistics.

Employment: Paralegal is a career with high growth potential; the Bureau of Labor Statistics forecrast an increase in jobs in the field of 27 percent or more through 2014, much faster than the average for all occupations.

Education: Most starting paralegals have an associate's degree in paralegal studies, which provides instruction in law, writing and research skills, and general education.

Work Environment: In corporate law firms, real estate law firms, and other offices in which a heavy work load requires the assistance of paralegals. Sometimes travel is necessary for research and other duties.

Paralegals assist lawyers in many capacities, such as aiding in research, preparing documents for court hearings, and organizing legal materials. Much like physicians' assistants, paralegals enable lawyers to do their jobs more efficiently, which saves valuable time and money. Paralegal work is a quickly expanding field with many opportunities for students who enjoy spending their time in libraries and in front of computers. About 224,000 paralegals were employed in 2004, a number that is expected to increase by nearly 30 percent by 2014.

Paralegals are also known as legal assistants, much as lawyers are often referred to as attorneys. The modern paralegal profession was created in the 1960s as a way to cut costs in order to provide legal services to the poor. Soon many law firms were employing paralegals to assist attorneys as they prepared for court, filed motions, and worked with clients. Today there are more than a quarter of a million paralegals working in the United States, and the profession is expanding rapidly to meet an increased demand.

While lawyers must attend law school and pass the bar exam to begin practicing law, educational requirements to become a paralegal include either an associate's degree in paralegal studies or a B.A. and certificate in paralegal studies. The National Federation of Paralegal Associations (NFPA) estimates that 25 percent of all paralegals have associate's degrees or a combination of a degree and certification. This can be obtained by passing an exam given by several paralegal associations. In addition to a degree in paralegal studies, experience is highly valued and can be obtained through internships and part-time positions.

Most paralegals are employed by private law firms, with the greatest opportunities existing at large firms in big cities. However, paralegals also are needed in smaller offices, at government agencies, and in community service organizations that provide legal assistance to clients ranging from the elderly to housing activists. A wide array of businesses also employs paralegals to support their in-house legal advisors. Real estate firms, banks, and insurance corporations are just a few places where you'll find paralegals working side by side with lawyers.

A paralegal's duties vary from the routine to the highly specialized, depending on the size of the company and the work that it does. For instance, a firm specializing in medical malpractice needs paralegals with strong backgrounds in the sciences to help prepare briefs and conduct research on medical issues. At smaller firms, paralegals need to be flexible and familiar with many different areas of the law, from the execution of wills to the filing of divorce agreements. Litigation is the area with the greatest growth for paralegals, as many Americans increasingly rely on the law to settle disputes.

Improvements in technology are another reason for the greater need for paralegals. While attorneys focus on their clients and caseloads, paralegals provide assistance with advanced computer databases, information retrieval systems, and law references online. The increased use of e-filing—the filing of legal documents online—has also resulted in a greater demand for paralegals, especially those familiar with that technology. One thing's for sure: If you decide to become a paralegal, you will be constantly improving and expanding your skills to keep up with the development of new technologies.

On the Job

Paralegals are employed everywhere law-related tasks are performed, including corporate law firms, government agencies, banks, insurance companies, and community service programs. In all cases, paralegals provide lawyers with aid ranging from clerical help to research support to interview assistance.

A starting place for many paralegals is as interns and in entry-level positions. In this capacity, new paralegals may be required to do a lot of clerical work such as filing, photocopying, and data entry. If you advance to a salaried position, you will become responsible for "coding," or numbering documents. "Bates stamping" is another duty you will encounter, and it also involves sequentially numbering or date/time marking images or documents as they are scanned or processed.

When you watch lawyers present cases on television, they often use exhibits and displays to make their points. Paralegals are sometimes responsible for putting these exhibits together. This may require advanced computer skills like knowledge of Photoshop or digital picture editing abilities. Other computer skills that are helpful include knowledge of Microsoft Office Suite Excel spreadsheets, PC Docs, Paradox, and Summation. The law is a field highly dependent on information of all kinds, so it is important to know how to find that information, organize it, and present it in a clear fashion.

Although most paralegals work a standard 40-hour week, often a heavy caseload requires additional hours in overtime. Some paralegals even work overnight shifts to meet deadlines. Such dedication may result in bonuses and perhaps even promotion. Responsibilities of more experienced paralegals include greater involvement in trial preparation, in which seasoned workers supervise and direct the newer members of the team. At the most senior level, paralegals become involved in the strategic side of the legal work, meeting with clients and helping to file motions and progress reports.

> **"It's always exciting, very challenging, and very rewarding. The clients they help and the people they get to know are the reasons paralegals like the work. They really help people."**
> —Charlotte DesHotels,
> **university paralegal studies coordinator**

Keys to Success

To be a successful paralegal, you should have

- research and investigative skills
- analytical abilities
- computer know-how
- ethical standards
- interest in law and legal issues
- time-management skills

Do You Have What It Takes?

Students interested in a career as a paralegal should enjoy doing research and using the Internet to uncover specialized information. High school courses that require intensive research will help you learn how to use the library as well as the Internet. Paralegals must be able to write well because they often help lawyers prepare reports and briefs, so focus on polishing your writing and grammar skills in high school. Computers are increasingly important in the legal world, so you should be familiar with how to use databases and various kinds of software.

A Typical Day at Work

A typical day for a paralegal might begin with an assignment from an attorney to research the legal precedents on a case the firm is representing. Perhaps a client is suing a large fast-food franchise because the franchise claimed their French fries were vegetarian, but they had been cooked in animal fat. You may do this research on your own or with a team of other paralegals, using the office's law library or perhaps Internet resources. When you complete your assignment, you must write a report on your findings, detailing the cases you uncovered, and perhaps providing copies of the laws. You may be the attorneys' liaison to the client, so it may fall upon you to report your findings and update the client about the status of the case. Your work will assist not only the lawyers presenting this case, but also those who have been affected by the franchise's false representation of its product. In this way, you have a direct impact on your client's case and a role in the law as well.

In addition to your other duties, if you are not working on a specific case, you may assist in interviews and attend real estate closings, depositions, or even trials, in which you will be relied on to provide necessary documents and take notes. If you work with a community service law organization, you will advocate for clients such as the handicapped and work with them from an initial interview through the completion of their cases. You will be supervised by an attorney but will be expected to conduct much of the work independently.

How to Break In

Internships often lead to employment for aspiring paralegals. They not only provide an opportunity for on-the-job training, but they also offer a chance to show that you can be a valuable addition to a firm. You can begin interning while still in high school at some firms, although your duties will be limited. As you work on your associate's degree, your responsibilities will increase. By the time you graduate, your job experience will match your training and help make you a more desirable job applicant.

Specializing in an area such as bankruptcy or intellectual property law can often lead to greater opportunities; companies sometimes land assignments that require a larger team of people trained in one area. Although this work may be only temporary, it may help you gain a full-time position. Computer savvy is always appreciated, so make sure to develop your understanding of databases and software programs, either through courses or on your own.

Two-Year Training

Although there is no formal licensing for paralegals, 85 percent of all paralegals receive some formal paralegal education, either certification or an associate's degree. Specialized courses include litigation, contract and tort law, intellectual property, and legal research and analysis. Students in these associate's degree programs are often required to maintain a minimum grade point average (GPA).

Nearly 1,000 schools offer training in paralegal studies. Of these, approximately 260 are approved by the American Bar Association (ABA), the organization that certifies attorneys. Competition for entrance to these schools is high, so you should have an excellent GPA and a transcript that includes challenging courses. Standardized tests and personal interviews are often required for entrance to ABA-approved schools. Students who graduate from ABA-approved programs have an advantage in the marketplace.

As the paralegal field becomes more specialized, so does the training. You may choose to concentrate your studies in an area of the law, such as bankruptcy. However, make sure to also have a fully rounded background in the law so that you can have many options available when you graduate. After a few years on the job, you may choose to further improve your résumé by earning a voluntary certification from the National Association of Legal Assistants (NALA). If you pass this two-day exam, you will receive the certified legal assistant (CLA) credential and potentially command a higher salary.

What to Look For in a School

When considering a two-year school, be sure to ask these questions:

☞ Will this degree program provide both course work and the connections to an internship?

☞ What is the school's job placement rate?

☞ Which areas of specialization does the school offer in paralegal studies?

☞ What are the professors' credentials? Have they worked in the industry? How available are the professors outside the classroom?

☞ Is the school ABA approved?

Interview with a Professional:
Q &A

Michelle Vicidomini

Paralegal, Law Offices of Daniel A. Thomas, P.C.,
New York, New York

Q: *How did you get started?*

A: I started my career as an intern while finishing my senior year of paralegal school. I received my degree in Paralegal Studies from New York Career Institute. I interned at my current job for two months before I was offered a full-time position. I've been working here for six years now.

Q: *What's a typical day like?*

A: Since I work for a small law office, just one attorney and myself, my day is never typical. It can vary from a full day of contacting the courts and speaking with the clerks, law secretaries, and even judges to reviewing records, responding to requests, and scheduling depositions, meetings, and court conferences. Each day brings a new and different experience.

Q: *What's your advice for those starting a career?*

A: My advice for those starting a career is to be assertive. Don't be afraid to ask questions if you don't know the answer: The law is constantly changing; what is valid today can be invalid tomorrow. It's important to be able to handle many tasks simultaneously and to do them efficiently and effectively by being organized. The law is very time-sensitive; therefore, it's extremely important for a paralegal to be aware of any and all deadlines and to keep the attorneys aware of the same. Keep in mind that the more experience you have, the more work and responsibility you will be given to complete on your own.

Q: *What's the best part of being a paralegal?*

A: The best part of being a paralegal for me is the feeling that I'm making a difference in people's lives. Since the law office is small, I get the opportunity to develop a great working relationship with our clients. Therefore, I'm able to see the results of my hard work firsthand through their appreciation and kindness.

Did You Know?

Funny lady Ellen DeGeneres, host of her own daytime show, *The Ellen De-Generes Show,* was a paralegal before making it as a comedienne.

The Future

Americans' increased reliance on legal solutions has resulted in a greater demand for lawyers and the services they provide. More and more, lawyers are turning to paralegals to assist them. As a result, the paralegal profession is expected to grow at a much faster than average rate in the next seven years. This is especially true as areas such as health care, international law, and medical malpractice also continue to expand. The best opportunities will be with large private law firms in big cities, although more and more banks, real estate firms, and insurance companies are turning to paralegals. In addition, community legal-service programs, which aid minorities, senior citizens, and the poor, will increasingly rely on the more economical services of paralegals to cut costs.

Job Seeking Tips

See the suggestions below and turn to Appendix A for advice on résumés and interviews.

✔ Decide what you're interested in and seek relevant experience.

✔ Talk to the career placement office at your school.

✔ If one area of the law really interests you, take courses or seminars to deepen your knowledge.

✔ Speak to people you know working as attorneys, paralegals, and legal secretaries for advice and job leads.

Career Connections

For further information, contact the following organizations.

The National Association of Legal Assistants http://www.nala.org

The National Federation of Paralegal Associations http://www .paralegals.org

Legal Assistant Today http://www.legalassistanttoday.com

American Bar Association Directory of ABA-Approved Paralegal Education Programs http://www.abanet.org/legalservices/paralegals/directory/allprograms.html

Associate's Degree Programs

Here are a few schools offering quality, ABA-approved paralegal programs:

Coastline Community College, Fountain Valley, California

Faulkner University, Montgomery, Alabama

Pennsylvania College of Technology, Williamsport, Pennsylvania
Center for Advanced Legal Studies, Houston, Texas

Financial Aid

Here is a paralegal-related scholarship. For more on financial aid for two-year students, turn to Appendix B.

Free Application for Federal Student Aid http://www.fafsa.ed.gov

Related Careers

Law clerk, title examiner, abstractor, claims adjuster, appraiser, and examiner.

Patrol Officer

Vital Statistics

Salary: Patrol officers average an annual salary of about $45,000 although their earnings often exceed this amount, in part because of overtime pay and benefits, according to 2006 data from the U.S. Bureau of Labor Statistics.

Employment: Law enforcement employment is forecast to grow about as fast as the average for all occupations through 2014, according to the Bureau of Labor Statistics.

Education: A two-year degree in criminal justice or police studies provides the knowledge of the law and police procedure as well as the necessary preparation for the required civil service exam.

Work Environment: The field of law enforcement can take patrol officers from the rugged edges of our nation's borders to highly populated city streets.

While most of us run away from trouble, those in law enforcement often find themselves running toward it. Whether responding to a call for help or intervening in a marital dispute, the people who enforce our laws put their lives in harm's way to assist others and maintain peace and order.

If you think you'd like to be a member of the team that protects our communities, there are many different kinds of law enforcement positions to consider, with uniformed police work being the most common. In fact, even those who patrol our cities' parks and beaches also work in law enforcement. So do fish and game wardens, border patrol agents, customs and immigration officials, transportation police, and canine corps members. As of 2004, there were more than 600,000 police and sheriff's patrol officers, a number that is expected to increase by more than 15 percent over the next seven years. For everyone who works in such a job, no two days are ever the same—and although completing paperwork is essential, a good portion of officers' time is spent far from their desks.

Instead, they may spend the day patrolling their beat in a squad car or on bicycle. Perhaps they monitor our nation's borders in an all-terrain vehicle to make sure no one enters the United States illegally. Some people in law enforcement may even have the enviable position of spending all day on a beautiful lake or river, making sure that nothing unlawful occurs.

Regardless of the setting, much of the job focuses on constant awareness and observation. David Ziskin, retired police officer of 20 years, writes about this aspect of the job in his book, *The Real Police:* "I loved patrolling.

It's sort of like hunting and sort of like relaxing all at the same time. . . . At least half of patrolling is the art of noticing things."

However, the job certainly does not end there. In fact, it often begins with a hunch or a suspicion that something is not right. Then it is the law enforcement official's duty to investigate and respond accordingly. Sometimes a simple warning to an offending party is enough. Other times, a suspect may flee, and must be pursued and apprehended. At all times, law enforcement officials must follow strict guidelines as they assist the law-abiding public and contend with people on the wrong side of the law. The notes and reports that officers file must be thorough and exact, so excellent communication skills and the ability to clearly express things in writing are also essential to the job.

While those in law enforcement must be physically fit, they must be mentally tough as well. On the job, they may need to engage in many disturbing incidents, such as a gun battle or a violent fist fight. They may respond to the scene of a car accident and need to take statements from witnesses, or be the first person to speak to a rape victim. Within a matter of seconds, those in law enforcement need to be able to exert force without hesitation. They also must be able to console the victims of crimes and their families and help them make clear statements so that justice can be achieved.

On the Job

All law enforcement employees are civil servants and are required to pass the civil service exam in their area. After candidates successfully pass the written examination, they also must pass oral interviews, psychological and background tests, drug and alcohol screening, and medical and physical agility tests. Then they attend a training academy, usually for 12 to 14 weeks. Here they learn about proper police procedure, constitutional law and regulations governing searches, arrests, and treatment of suspects. They also receive training in firearms, self-defense, and first aid. If they successfully complete the academy and meet all other requirements in their state, they begin work as rookies.

Many types of law enforcement work are done in shifts, for 24-hour protection and surveillance are essential in all of our communities. This can be very difficult at times because the "graveyard shift" is either full of illegal activity and arrests, or in smaller, more rural areas, very dull. Rookies are often assigned the least desirable shifts, either working late or overnight. However, they are usually partnered with more experienced veterans who mentor them on the job.

Overtime is another typical component of law enforcement because special assignments, additional training, and court appearances make 40-hour work weeks highly unusual. Communication skills and organization are very important because law enforcers write and file reports on incidents that occurred during their shifts and handle other administrative paperwork.

Those in law enforcement are responsible for their districts or areas that their department covers. Officers must be highly familiar with the layout of their district so that they can respond quickly to calls and anticipate the location and the direction a suspect may be heading. They must know the law inside and out and follow it at all times so that when a case is built, no mistakes have been made that might jeopardize the outcome.

> **"I've had 13 years on the job, and one of the best assignments I've had was as a youth officer. . . . I can't think of another profession that would make me prouder."**
> —Yvette Irizarry, police officer, New York Police Department

Keys to Success

To be successful in law enforcement, you should have

- a strong sense of responsibility
- physical stamina
- sound judgment
- a desire to help others
- excellent observation skills
- a clean record

Do You Have What It Takes?

Students who are interested in law enforcement should be honest, fair-minded, and willing to put their lives in danger to protect others. You must always be alert to potential danger or unlawful activity and willing to do what it takes to enforce the law, including use extreme force if the situation requires it. A good level of physical fitness is very important for a patrol officer, as is the ability to always obey the law. You should have a strong respect for authority, for you will be required to follow the commands of your superior officers at all times. Good note-taking is another important aspect of the job; you'll need to rely on these notes if you have to testify in court.

A Typical Day at Work

Typical days vary depending on your assignment. This week, you are on the "graveyard shift," patrolling your precinct in your squad car. At 3:30 a.m., just as you're about to stop for coffee, a call comes in that a neighborhood convenience store has just been robbed. You turn on the siren and lights and head for the crime scene. When you arrive, the clerk, visibly shaken but unharmed, tries to unravel the chain of events but is too upset to make any sense. You slowly lead him through a series of questions that calm him down and enable him to describe everything he remembers. As you take notes on his responses, your partner retrieves video from the surveillance camera to see if the perpetrator has been caught on tape. You and your partner then search the perimeter of the store. Returning to the squad car, you drive slowly along adjacent streets, scanning carefully for suspicious pedestrians. Your partner spots several teenagers huddled under the bleachers in the town baseball field. As you get out of the car to question them, two of them take off across the field, outrunning you and your partner until one of them twists his ankles and falls down. Already smelling the alcohol on his breath, you cuff him and lead him back to the car so you can take him to the station for questioning. Before the close of your shift, you will write up all that has transpired on this and other calls.

How to Break In

If you know you want to work in law enforcement, get started in high school by becoming involved with an Explorers unit, run by the Boy Scouts of America. These groups learn about things such as firearms and canine divisions. Forces in major cities often hire recent high school graduates still in their teens as police cadets or trainees. These trainees do clerical work and attend classes until they meet the age requirement. The military is another avenue to a career in law enforcement. If you know what type of enforcement you'd like to specialize in, prepare yourself by learning the requirements for service and begin any training you can in advance.

Two-Year Training

While some departments may require college-level coursework, even those that don't take notice of the additional training a two-year degree provides. It makes candidates stand out in more competitive areas such as highway patrol and positions in more affluent areas. Nearly half of the officers between ages 25 and 44 have some college credits. Two-year associate's degrees in criminal justice, police studies, and law enforcement provide a good foundation for both the civil service exam and work in the field.

Courses in constitutional law, civil rights, composition, and accounting prepare students for future positions in law enforcement. Other courses, such as cross-cultural studies or foreign languages, can prepare students for work with diverse populations and enable them to empathize with those they serve as well as communicate more clearly.

Most law enforcement agencies have a minimum age requirement. You can start your degree while you wait to qualify for training. Promotion in many law enforcement fields is based on job performance and seniority as well as a written and/or oral interview, but a two-year degree will help prepare you to perform better on the job and in front of your superior officers.

What to Look For in a School

When considering a two-year school, be sure to ask these questions:

☞ Will the school's curriculum help me pass the civil service exam?

☞ Will this degree program provide me with both theoretical and practical knowledge for the job?

☞ What are the instructors' credentials? Have they worked as police officers or in other areas of protective services?

☞ Does the school offer computer training relevant to law enforcement work?

☞ What kind of relationship does the school have with the local law enforcement community? Does the school arrange internships?

The Future

Positions in law enforcement are expected to increase in the coming years as more and more officers take advantage of early retirement options that enable them to retire at half pay and pursue second careers while still in their forties or fifties. The public's increasing concern with safety after 9/11 is another reason that law enforcement will expand, as are rising concerns about illegal immigration and drug-related crimes. The best opportunities will be in urban areas with higher crime rates and large forces as well as in specialized areas of law enforcement. Those with postsecondary education will have an advantage in this highly competitive field.

Did You Know?

Basketball superstar Shaquille O'Neal was a reserve officer with the Los Angeles Port Police and then a reserve officer with the Miami police force.

Interview with a Professional:
Q &A
Kristin Harrison
Patrol officer, Boston College Police Department,
Chestnut Hill, Massachusetts

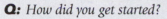

Q: *How did you get started?*

A: I developed an interest in law enforcement when I was in an administrative support position, working for a former FBI agent. He thought I'd be good at law enforcement and urged me to look into it. I took a couple of classes in criminal justice at Northeastern University's extension school. I liked the classes so much that I went back to school full time and got a degree in criminal justice.

Q: *What's a typical day like?*

A: We start with roll call, where they check attendance, assign us to a cruiser and a sector, and discuss incidents that occurred in the previous two shifts. The bulk of the day's work could be motor vehicle enforcement, taking reports of a minor nature such as lost or found property, a foot chase with a suspect, or an investigation into a sexual assault. I never really know, which makes this job exciting.

Q: *What's your advice for those starting a career?*

A: Get to know the profession. Many cities and towns allow civilians to ride around with an officer and learn from watching and from asking questions. They might also give you advice as to which departments in the area are the better ones to work for. No matter what you do to get your foot in the door, you should always keep your eyes open and your mouth shut. Learning the ropes in law enforcement is best done by observing, asking questions, showing enthusiasm, and reserving your opinion. The more you are able to do this in the beginning of your career, the better officer you will be.

Q: *What's the best part of being a law enforcer?*

A: The pride and satisfaction you get when you're able to improve a person's quality of life brings immediate gratification. The other great thing is the adrenaline rush. I'm happy to dole out directions in exchange for an occasional adrenaline-raising moment. That's how I know that I'm in the right profession—I even love the boring moments.

Job Seeking Tips

See the suggestions below and turn to Appendix A for advice on résumés and interviews.

✔ Always be well groomed and neatly dressed when you appear for an interview or training; show respectful manners.

✔ Maintain a clean driving record and stay away from drug use of any kind.

✔ Take some courses in useful fields such as accounting, English composition, and foreign languages.

✔ Follow leads in several different areas. The application process is both lengthy and highly competitive, so it's good to have alternatives.

✔ Know when applications are being accepted as well as when the civil service exams are given.

Career Connections

For further information, contact the following organizations.

Law Enforcement Jobs.com http://www.lawenforcementjobs.com

Officer.com http://www.officer.com

Policetraining.net http://www.policetraining.net

Learning for Life http://www.learning-for-life.org/exploring/lawenforcement/index.html

Associate's Degree Programs

Here are a few schools offering quality criminal justice or police studies programs:

Bitonte College of Health and Human Services—Youngstown State University, Youngstown, Ohio

City Colleges of Chicago, Chicago, Illinois

Eagle Gate College, Layton, Murray, and Salt Lake City, in Utah

John Jay College of Criminal Justice, New York, New York

Financial Aid

Here are a few law enforcement–related scholarships. For more on financial aid for two-year students, turn to Appendix B.

National Black Police Association http://www.blackpolice.org/Scholarship.html

The following Exploring Scholarships and Awards are for youths participating in the **Learning for Life** or **Explorer** program (http://www.learning-for-life.org/exploring/scholarships/index.html).

National Youth Representative Scholarship Law Enforcement Exploring provides a scholarship to the outgoing national youth representative at the National Law Enforcement Conference.

ATFAR Scholarship The retiree's association of the Bureau of Alcohol, Tobacco, Firearms and Explosives (ATF) offers scholarships of $1,000 to Law Enforcement Explorers.

The National Technical Investigators Association presents two Capt. James J. Regan Scholarships, one-time $500 awards, annually. Criteria include academic record, leadership, extracurricular activities, and a personal statement.

Sheryl A. Horak Memorial Scholarship This merit-based award involves a $1,000 one-time scholarship. The award also includes a plaque and pin.

Related Careers

Private detective, investigator, corrections officer, security officer, probation/parole officer, aviation security officer, emergency services personnel, crime scene analysis personnel, and drug enforcement officer.

Park Ranger

Park rangers wear many hats, from providing information to the public to protecting natural resources to enforcing laws and regulations in parks, historical buildings, and recreation sites across the country. All in all, it's a great job if you like to be active, work in nature, and help maintain and care for our nation's parks, lakes, mountains, and oceans.

In our country, we have national parks and forests, state and local parks, historical landmarks, and nature preserves and refuges. They all have different purposes and different rules and regulations. For example, national parks usually forbid hunting, while national forests allow it. In general, the rules governing parks are stricter than those governing forests, which are based on the idea of "multiple use," such as use for timber, cattle grazing, and mineral excavation.

Depending on where they work, rangers enforce different sets of laws. What's more, various locations also have different requirements for employment. Although many National Parks Service positions look for candidates with four-year degrees, it is possible to be hired with only a two-year degree, especially if you have relevant volunteer experience in parks work or conservation. Requirements at state and local parks vary, so it is best to decide where you want to work and then find out what kind of degree and experience are needed.

Wherever you work, your job will involve protecting wildlife and natural resources. You will also be protecting those who come to enjoy those natural resources, such as campers, hikers, and fishermen. You will need to know basic first aid, if not more advanced lifesaving techniques. Since you will be responsible for monitoring the whereabouts of hikers and campers, you will often be the first to know if a party is in trouble, and you will organize a search-and-rescue mission.

Other tasks you'll need to complete as a ranger include restocking fire-wood, directing traffic, and testing water supplies. You will need to maintain any equipment you use, such as chain saws, all-terrain vehicles, and office machines. You should be adaptable enough to accomplish all of your duties, from the most exciting to the most ordinary, and you should be prepared for anything on your shift, from bear activity to a power outage.

As you gain more and more experience, you may decide to focus on one of the four main types of ranger work: law enforcement, resources management, administration, and interpretation, which involves educational work. Whatever you choose, no two days will be the same.

On the Job

Safety is your number one concern as a park ranger. Much like a police officer, you enforce the laws governing the land and take appropriate action when those laws are violated. Some rangers carry firearms, while others do not: It depends on the location and risk involved in the area. Sometimes wildlife may pose a significant threat, and rangers must be able to protect themselves and others from violent predators. Monitoring these threats is just part of what rangers do. Other duties include trail maintenance, resource management, and forest-fire patrol. Should a fire be spotted, rangers work as firefighters, tending the blaze until other firefighters arrive.

Entry-level rangers are often initially assigned desk work. This time provides a chance to develop your leadership skills as well as build your knowledge. You will be fielding many questions from visitors about regulations, directions, and wildlife, so take the time to learn what you need to know for your particular park or forest. You may discover that you want to specialize in one area, such as fish and wildlife or law enforcement. Acquire all the knowledge you can to put yourself ahead in your chosen field.

A majority of park work is solitary. Very often, no one is going to tell you what to do; you must decide for yourself where the work is and set priorities. If you discover that a tree has fallen on a trail, it will be your responsibility to make sure it is cleared. Similarly, if a fishing party is not following the regulations or fishing without licenses, it will be up to you to confront them and issue either a violation or a warning. Park rangers enforce the law, so make sure you're comfortable with confrontation.

Keys to Success

To be a successful park ranger, you should have
- the ability to react quickly in an emergency
- independent work habits
- a strong interest in the environment
- the ability to follow and give instructions

❧ good written and oral communication skills
❧ the ability to confront unlawful citizens

Do You Have What It Takes?

Students interested in a career as a park ranger should have a passion for the outdoors. They should also enjoy courses in biology and the life sciences, as well as mathematics and history. The job involves strenuous work, so you should be in good physical condition and feel comfortable being alone in the woods. Knowledge of cardiopulmonary resuscitation (CPR) and other first-aid techniques is valuable, as is the ability to read maps. While in high school, you can gain experience by joining organizations such as the Boy Scouts in the United States or Scouts Canada. The Student Conservation Association is another great volunteer organization that can expose you to opportunities in our nation's parks.

A Typical Day at Work

The variety of jobs available to park rangers is as diverse as parks themselves. Regardless of where you work, however, you will have certain responsibilities and duties. Many rangers work solo, so you must be good at budgeting time and prioritizing tasks.

A typical day begins by checking the logbook to see if any maintenance jobs need to be completed, such as repairing a fence or removing a fallen tree from a footpath. After you've worked up a sweat, it's off to the information booth, where you greet park visitors, answer questions about the facility, or give directions. Then you'll assist at the nature center, where you'll give a talk about the park's wildlife, especially the family of bears that has recently been spotted eating a visitor's leftovers. Patrol duty is next, so you'll jump on your all-terrain vehicle to check fishing licenses and make sure park rules and regulations are being followed. You may need to issue a violation to visitors who have failed to remove their trash or snowmobilers who have strayed from the assigned trails. Some visitors do not respect wildlife and may enter protected nesting grounds or damage an at-risk habitat. All of these incidents need to be dealt with and reported, both to your superior officer and in the logbook, where you list infractions, unusual occurrences, and even bear sightings.

How to Break In

One of the best ways to become a park ranger is to spend your summer vacations in related work. This may include jobs as a camp counselor, nature preserve guide, or volunteer at a local park. Organizations like Green

Corps, the Sierra Club, and the Appalachian Trail Conservancy can provide valuable volunteer experience and connections to temporary and permanent positions. Positions as campground hosts and trail maintainers are excellent ways to build your résumé and make contacts in the field. If you find a place you'd like to work, see if they offer internships and ask what kind of training they require of full-time employees. Currently, the National Park System has 140,000 volunteers helping its 20,000 permanent, temporary, and seasonal workers, so volunteering is clearly a great way to break in to this exciting field.

> **"In hiring, I look for the basics. I think someone should have honesty, integrity, and the ability to communicate—to relate to others. Especially important, though, is a positive outlook on life and an ability to learn."**
> **—Thomas D. Ambrose, assistant superintendent, Cacapon State Park, West Virginia**

Two-Year Training

There are many different two-year programs that will prepare you for work as a park ranger. These include parks and recreation management, forest technology, and park ranger technology. The majority of these programs are located in fairly rural settings where fieldwork can take place. Competition is fierce, so prepare yourself by taking as many relevant courses as you can. These include biology, botany, conservation, forest management, and CPR.

You should also develop skills outside the classroom. Learn how to use Global Positioning System (GPS) navigation, or at least how to use a compass, and make sure your map-reading skills are well tuned. A few courses in outdoor sports such as rock climbing and white water rafting will make you a more appealing candidate as well, and will also increase your confidence when in the wilderness.

If you decide to specialize in law enforcement, the Seasonal Law Enforcement Training Program (SLETP) consists of 334 class hours and is another excellent way to improve your résumé and improve your chances for advancement. After completion of the course and the necessary background check, you will be eligible to receive a type II law enforcement commission, which will enable you to carry a gun, make arrests, and investigate crimes. More information on this program can be found on the Association of National park rangers' Web site at http://www.anpr.org/academies.htm.

What to Look For in a School

When considering a two-year school, be sure to ask these questions:

☞ Will this degree program provide both course work and the connections to an internship?

☞ What is the school's job placement rate?

☞ What are the professors' credentials? Have they worked in the field? How available are the professors outside the classroom?

☞ Will this degree enable me to obtain the ranger job I want? Will I be able to transfer credits to a four-year degree program?

☞ Does the program have a good balance of classroom hours and fieldwork?

☞ What kind of relationship does the school have with the national park and forest community?

The Future

In the coming years, there will continue to be openings in remote park settings. There will also be many opportunities for those interested in work as rangers in our urban parks and recreation areas as well because of the increase in the number and size of these facilities. As concern for the nation's natural resources continues to grow, there will be a greater need for professionals to oversee parklands and protect wildlife. This concern also means that there will be more interest in ranger positions, so competition will be strong. An associate's degree and seasonal work experience will help you rise above the pack.

Did You Know?

In the 1920s, Benton MacKaye, a U.S. Forest Service worker and wilderness advocate, was convinced that the pace of urban and industrial life was harmful. He envisioned the Appalachian Trail, which today stretches 2,175 miles from Maine to Georgia.

Interview with a Professional:
Q &A

Maya Seraphin

U.S. park ranger, Glacier Bay National Park and
Preserve, Alaska

Q: *How did you get started?*

A: I was lucky enough to grow up in a family that spent a lot of time hiking and backpacking. In high school, I volunteered with the Student Conservation Association (SCA) and built trails in the back country of Yosemite National Park in California. In college, I volunteered with SCA in Olympic National Park in Washington. My two summers working alongside National Park Service employees inspired me to pursue a career as a park ranger. I worked as a fee collector and ranger naturalist before going into law enforcement.

Q: *What's a typical day like?*

A: My job boils down to protecting the park from the people, the people from the park, and the people from the people. An average day may involve investigating a motor vehicle accident, treating a sprained ankle or possible heart attack, patrolling by boat to check fishing licenses and enforce wildlife closures, teaching CPR/first aid to fellow National Park Service employees, coordinating an oil spill response drill, responding to a reported wildfire, or managing visitors around a foraging black bear with cubs.

Q: *What's your advice for those starting a career?*

A: Volunteering in a park is the best way to get an idea of what kind of work is available. Enjoying people, being flexible, and believing in what you do are important qualities to bring to the job.

Q: *What's the best part of being a park ranger?*

A: The best part of my job is that I'm involved in helping protect something irreplaceable as a public servant for the American public. As a law enforcement officer, I have a full range of options to do this. Much of my job is still education, but I also have other tools, such as issuing tickets and arrest authority, at my disposal if the situation warrants.

Job Seeking Tips

See the suggestions below and turn to Appendix A for advice on résumés and interviews.

✔ Decide what you're interested in and seek relevant experience.

✔ Talk to the career placement office about opportunities locally and in other states.

✔ Develop skills such as orienteering, CPR, and first aid.

✔ Volunteer at a state or local park.

✔ Become familiar with area plants and wildlife through field guides or classes.

✔ Join a nature conservancy or wilderness organization to learn more about our country's natural resources and get involved in preserving them.

Career Connections

For further information, contact the following organizations.

Student Conservation Association http://www.thesca.org

Seasonal Employment Program, National Park Service http://www.sep.nps.gov

Park Ranger.com http://www.parkranger.com/jobsresultsold.htm

Association of National Park Rangers http://www.anpr.org

The National Park Service http://www.nps.gov

USDA Forest Service http://www.fs.fed.us/fsjobs

Sierra Club http://www.sierraclub.org

Appalachian Trail Conservancy http://www.appalachiantrail.org

Green Corps http://www.greencorps.org

Associate's Degree Programs

Here are a few schools offering quality park ranger programs:

SUNY-ESF, Syracuse, New York

Colorado Northwestern Community College, Rangely, Colorado

Hocking College, Nelsonville, Ohio

Wayne Community College, Goldsboro, North Carolina

Financial Aid

Here is a park ranger–related scholarship. For more on financial aid for two-year students, turn to Appendix B.

National Park Service http://www.nps.gov/training/develop.htm

Related Careers

Law enforcement officer, wildlife-management personnel, zookeeper, landscaper, and pollution-containment personnel.

Paramedic/ Emergency Medical Technician

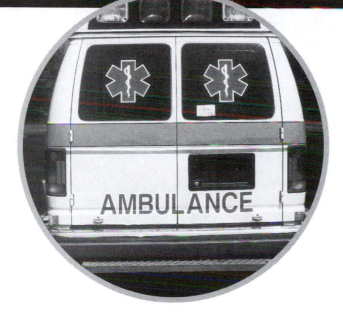

Vital Statistics

Salary: Average salaries vary based on location and experience. The median salary for paramedics and emergency medical technicians (EMTs) is $25,310, according to 2006 data from the U.S. Bureau of Labor Statistics.

Employment: EMTs and paramedics should enjoy job growth that is much faster than the average for all occupations through 2014, according to the Bureau of Labor Statistics.

Education: An associate's degree in emergency medical technology provides preparation for both the practical and written portions of the National Registry of Emergency Medical Technicians (NREMT) exam required by 43 states, or its equivalent.

Work Environment: EMTs and paramedics work at accident and medical emergency scenes. They also work in ambulances en route to their hospital, and occasionally in the emergency rooms.

If you've ever watched TV shows like *E.R.* or *Grey's Anatomy,* you've probably seen the uniformed technicians who deliver patients to emergency room doctors. These are emergency medical technicians (EMTs) or paramedics, dedicated professionals responsible for pre-hospital emergency care. Emergency medical services (EMS) is an exciting field, filled with life-and-death moments that provide great job satisfaction as well as the chance to help others in their most critical moments.

EMS work is not for the timid. As first responders, EMTs and paramedics are often the earliest to arrive at car accidents, drownings, or violent crime scenes. They must quickly assess the nature and extent of a patient's condition, determine whether there are pre-existing medical concerns, administer care, and prepare the patient for transfer to the hospital should that be necessary. In the ambulance, they must drive safely and quickly to the appropriate facility as well as tend to the patient, communicate with accompanying family members, and—at the same time—exchange information with other medical professionals and follow their instructions should the need arise for more complex care.

Napoleon Bonaparte first systematized patient care in the early 1800s, beginning with soldiers on the battlefield. At that time, the fundamentals of emergency care were established. These include swift response to those in need by trained medical personnel, immediate treatment and stabilization, and delivery to a local hospital or medical facility while care is provided.

Emergency medicine, of course, has vastly improved from those distant battlefield days. In the past, patients were merely brought to the back door of the hospital by "ambulance drivers" who had no medical training. There, they were met by whatever physician was on duty. Today, doctors specialize in emergency medicine, and although patients are still delivered to the back door of most hospitals because of tradition, their care is far superior to that of the past. That care begins with the EMTs and paramedics who respond to 9-1-1 calls.

EMTs and paramedics may work for a public or private ambulance service or as part of a fire or police department or as part of a hospital team. They may also work in a private-care facility such as a convalescent home. More populated areas tend to place more EMS calls, and increasingly people are relying on EMS teams to respond to nonemergency medical conditions. This dependence puts a strain on EMS forces and often results in the establishment of private ambulance companies in areas that can financially support them. These private companies are often used to transport patients in nonemergency situations when medical oversight is still required, such as the transfer of patients from nursing homes to hospitals prior to operations.

EMT training begins with EMT-Basic, the first level of technical knowledge where all EMTs begin. Once you have passed your practical training, you will spend time riding with a crew or in an emergency room. To advance to EMT-Intermediate or EMT-Paramedic, your continued classroom training must be supplemented by time in the field, much as doctors have to serve residencies to become fully certified.

On the Job

EMTs and paramedics work wherever an accident, injury, or critical health condition occurs. They must be prepared for every possibility, from a patient who has severed a finger to a woman giving birth. They may be based at a firehouse or hospital, or simply be *on call*, which means that they must monitor an emergency radio or carry a beeper and respond if a call is in their area.

These calls, of course, can occur during the middle of the night, important family dinners, or major holidays. If you are on call, you must abandon whatever you are doing and go to the scene to assist and follow a *decision tree*, the strict protocol used to prioritize care. You will begin by quickly assessing the patient's status, using devices such as stethoscopes and blood pressure monitors. Precautions must be taken to avoid communicable diseases such as HIV or TB through the use of gloves and face masks. You'll also need to check for pre-existing medical conditions such as diabetes or epilepsy, find out what prescription medications the patient is on, and decide if the patient's condition requires a visit to the emergency room

If transport is required, you must check for potential breaks, stabilize the patient by placing him or her on either a stretcher or backboard, and safely move the patient to the ambulance. One EMT drives while the other stays with the patient and continues to provide care, often under the direction of hospital physicians who are communicating from the emergency room.

Once you arrive at the ER, you will need to quickly and clearly convey the patient's vital statistics and describe the trauma that occurred. You may also need to continue to provide assistance to the ER staff as they administer to the patient.

When your call is over, you are responsible for disinfecting your car and replacing all used resources, such as splints and bandages. Your work is both physically and mentally demanding, since you are often required to kneel, bend, and do heavy lifting as well as transport and treat both physically and mentally distressed victims. You may also face physical danger as you deal with unstable patients or violent experiences such as shootings. Some days at work will pass with no calls, while others may be filled with life-threatening situations and traumas.

> **"It's a job that is very real, very exciting, sometimes dangerous, but never easy. You'll see people on some of the worst and some of the best days of their lives."**
> —Toronto EMS chief, Bruce Farr, in *Toronto Sun*

Keys to Success

To be a successful EMT/paramedic, you should have

- the desire to help others
- physical and emotional stamina
- excellent communication skills
- quick decision-making abilities
- common sense
- the ability to stay cool under pressure

Do You Have What It Takes?

Students who are interested in a career as an EMT/paramedic need to be comfortable dealing with people who are often in great physical and mental distress. The job requires that you pass both a written and a practical exam, which involves a lot of memorization of specialized medical information. This means students interested in this field should be strong in science, as well as hard working in their studies. You must be in good physical condition so you can help your patients either by lifting them onto stretchers or restraining those who are in great distress.

Again, this job is not for the faint of heart. If you like helping others and respond well in a crisis, emergency medical services may be for you. Be prepared to work irregular hours in settings from the living room of an elderly heart attack patient to a six-lane highway where a five-car pile-up has resulted in multiple victims.

A Typical Day at Work

You're out bowling when your cell phone rings: There's a three-car accident by the high school. It doesn't sound good. When you arrive, two ambulances from your company are already there. You grab your gloves, protective eyewear, and face mask, and head for the center of the accident. Two teenage girls are sitting by the side of the road, crying. Your chief tells you to check their vitals and examine them for injuries. As you take one girl's blood pressure, put a stethoscope to her chest, and shine a penlight in her eyes, you are relieved to see that she is okay. You repeat the same steps with her friend, who is also fine, just badly shaken. You hand them a blanket to cover up with since they are cold and head to an SUV that is badly damaged. You're told that an elderly man is still trapped inside, but is conscious and alert. You've developed a reputation on the squad for calming people down, so as the firemen work to cut through the passenger-side door, you step up to the driver's window and make eye contact with the victim. You ask him a few simple questions to distract him and ease his discomfort, and remember why you trained for this job.

How to Break In

Begin by getting certified in cardiopulmonary resuscitation (CPR) and learn basic lifesaving techniques. Volunteering in a hospital or nursing home is another way to gain valuable experience and add to your résumé. Some EMS providers even offer volunteer positions to high school students, who can do "ride-alongs" with ambulance crews as they respond to calls. Finally, develop an excellent knowledge of the roads in your area so that your driving skills will be yet another asset when you apply for an EMT position.

Courses in biology and human anatomy are obvious choices if you are considering a career in emergency medicine. Knowing a foreign language, such as Spanish, may be a huge advantage on the job; you could end up being the only member of your EMS team able to communicate with a patient.

Two-Year Training

Two-year training in emergency medical technology results in an associate's degree, which will make you stand out in a competitive field. Nearly 65 percent of EMS workers between the ages of 25 and 44 have some college education. An associate's degree will also prepare you to take the NREMT exam or the equivalent required exam in your state, but you must also complete clinical and fieldwork before you can be certified.

There are four levels of EMT training and certification, and you must start at EMT-Basic and work your way up from there through time in the field. EMT-Basic is the entry level and can be achieved by taking a six- to ten-week course totaling 110 to 120 hours at a local firehouse, hospital, or community college. Most firefighters are required to have this basic certification, which enables them to manage respiratory, cardiac, and trauma patients.

EMT-Intermediate, or EMT-II and -III, is achieved after an additional 200 to 400 hours in the classroom and the field. These technicians can administer intravenous fluids, use defibrillators (the apparatus that helps cardiac patients recover), and employ advanced airway techniques.

Paramedics are the most advanced of the emergency technicians. All paramedics must first practice as registered EMTs. This path requires extensive coursework in body function and advanced lifesaving techniques, as well as 500 to 2,000 hours in the field. Even with an associate's degree, you must complete this time in the field to become a paramedic. Because of the extent of paramedics' training, almost all are paid rather than volunteer positions.

What to Look For in a School

When considering a two-year school, be sure to ask these questions:

☞ Will the course prepare me to pass either the NREMT or the written and practical exams required in my state?

☞ What kind of relationship does the program have with area ambulance companies, hospitals, and fire departments? Are internships available through the school?

☞ What are the professors' credentials? Are the instructors either working EMTs and paramedics or retired from emergency services?

☞ Does the school offer career guidance and provide contacts for positions both in my area and beyond?

Interview with a Professional:
Q &A
Rachel Terranova
EMT-Basic, Alamo EMS, Dutchess County, New York

Q: *How did you get started?*

A: I took my emergency medical technician class at Vassar College. I always thought that it would be good to know how to do CPR and provide medical care because there are a lot of small children in my family. Halfway through the course, I realized that I could actually get paid to use these skills. I was hired soon after I received my New York State certification as an Emergency Medical Technician-Basic level.

Q: *What's a typical day like?*

A: The best part of the job is that no day is typical. I always check my equipment at the beginning of the shift and hand in my paperwork at the end, but everything in between is up for grabs. Every day brings different emergencies. Shifts are usually 8, 12, 16, or 24 hours, and my partner and I may be very busy or we may sit all day. Patients are treated and transported to the hospital, where we work with the nurses, techs, and doctors in the ER by giving them an idea of what has happened. Then we clean up and do it all over again for another patient in another situation.

Q: *What's your advice for those starting a career?*

A: Learn as much as you can from anyone who is willing to teach you. This is especially true in emergency medicine because 99 percent of your learning takes place on the job. The certification class is vital and will teach you many things, but experience is your best teacher.

Q: *What's the best part of being an EMT?*

A: When a patient's problem is not clear-cut and I have to think critically and draw on my knowledge and previous experience. Trying to figure out what might be causing someone's symptoms is like a puzzle you have to put together before you know what you can do to help.

Did You Know?

While training to became a paramedic in New York City, former Van Halen frontman David Lee Roth saved the life of a heart attack victim by using a defibrillator.

The Future

Turnover is high in emergency services because of the irregular hours and demanding and stressful work. As a result, there is always a need for new EMTs and paramedics. Competition is still intense, however, so your associate's degree will make you stand out. The Department of Labor expects this field to grow at a greater than average rate partially because of increased urbanization and development. In 2004, 192,000 people were employed in emergency medical services, a number that is expected to grow to 244,000 by 2014, an increase of more than 27 percent. Aging baby boomers are another reason this is a growing field; as they get older, they will experience more medical emergencies.

Job Seeking Tips

See the suggestions below and turn to Appendix A for advice on résumés and interviews.

✔ Find out the requirements in your state by calling a local EMS service or going online. Most states require that you pass the NREMT exam, while others administer their own tests.

✔ Maintain a clean driving record.

✔ Volunteer with your local ambulance service if possible.

✔ Network with local EMTs and paramedics and other friends seeking positions in emergency services.

✔ Surf the Internet for training tips and advice from EMTs and paramedics.

Career Connections

For further information on EMS, contact the following organizations.

National Association of Emergency Medical Technicians
http://www.naemt.org
National Registry of Emergency Medical Technicians
http://www.nremt.org
FiremanEMTParamedic.com http://www.firemanemtparamedic.com
EMSvillage http://www.emsvillage.com

Associate's Degree Programs

Here are a few schools with two-year EMS programs:
Lane Community College, Eugene, Oregon
Pima Community College, Tucson, Arizona

Kalamazoo Valley Community College, Kalamazoo, Michigan

Holmes Community College, Ridgeland, Mississippi

Financial Aid

Here are a few EMS scholarships. For information on financial aid for two-year students, turn to Appendix B.

FieldMedics.com http://www.fieldmedics.com/supportservices/scholarship.htm

National Association of EMTs http://www.naemt.org/awardsAndScholarships/EMTOfTheYear/

Kentucky EMS Connection http://www.hultgren.org/library/scholarship/index.html

Related Careers

EMT instructor, dispatcher, EMS supervisor, operations manager, director of emergency services, firefighter, helicopter rescue squad, physician assistant, and registered nurse.

Corrections
Officer

Vital Statistics

Salary: The median yearly salary for corrections officers is $33,600, according to 2006 data from the U.S. Bureau of Labor Statistics.

Employment: Corrections employment is projected to grow more slowly than the average for all occupations through 2014, due mainly to the rapid growth of recent decades and limitations on what states can afford, according to the Bureau of Labor Statistics.

Education: An associate's degree in criminal justice/corrections provides instruction in correctional theory and practice in addition to psychology and human behavior.

Work Environment: The work environment is mostly indoors in institutional prison settings, although some work occurs outdoors in the yards and exterior perimeters of the prison as well as in vehicles used for transporting inmates.

Americans spend a great deal of time following the pursuit and capture of criminals. We watch their exploits on TV and closely follow their trials and sentences. However, few people ever get the inside scoop about what happens once someone enters the system. Corrections officers, also referred to as COs, are in charge of the men and women who serve time in the prison system. The term *prison guard* has been replaced by this new title.

Prisons and jails are managed at the city, county, state, and federal levels. When suspects are arrested they are often held in local or city jails until they post bail—a fee that guarantees their appearance in court—or until they complete their trials. Those found guilty of certain felonies and sentenced to terms of one year or more are usually transferred to state prisons. Federal prisons hold those who have committed federal crimes, such as Internet child pornography or tax evasion. Currently, COs process and admit more than 11 million people a year in the U.S. jail system. Nearly half a million people are employed as COs: three out of five work in state facilities, while federal and privately run prisons employ approximately 16,000 people each. (Although most prisons are public institutions, some are privately run.)

The prison system has three levels of security: minimum, medium, and maximum. Nonviolent felons are usually sent to lower-security facilities, while violent and repeat offenders are sent to higher-security settings. A few ultra-max facilities exist for extremely dangerous inmates. The level of security varies from settings much like highly supervised communities with limited freedom to extremely restricted environments. Most state and federal prisons are located in rural, fairly isolated areas. City and county jails may be attached to courthouses or be in separate locations. Prison populations tend to be more stable than those of jails, which receive many different kinds of criminals, whose temperament and threat levels are unknown and therefore unpredictable.

For COs, workweeks are organized in shifts. After all, supervision is needed 24 hours a day, seven days a week. Only the most senior officers are able to avoid night and holiday shifts. Responsibilities include supervising inmates, overseeing the intake and transfer of admissions, maintaining the security of the facility inside and out, keeping daily logs of inmate activity, and filing reports when needed. Officers must also inspect visitors and all packages and mail that arrive.

Correctional positions offer better benefits and job security than noncorrectional work as facilities strive to maintain their staffs and compensate for rural locations and shift work. Increased responsibilities and salary are possible through seniority and job performance. Correctional treatment specialists (who work one-on-one with inmates in a therapeutic setting), strategic deployment forces, and wardens often begin as officers and work their way up to positions of greater specialization and authority. To qualify for a position as a CO, applicants undergo physical and psychological testing, interviews, background checks, and a state or federally administered written exam on prison policies, how to manage inmates, and basic legal terms. Drug and alcohol testing is also common.

On the Job

Corrections work can be very stressful and even dangerous, but COs enjoy the chance to protect their communities. COs must maintain order and security within their facility at all times. They do this by establishing a consistent routine and also through the withdrawal of inmate privileges. Officers must be fair-minded and even-tempered, as inmates often try to manipulate them and test their resolve. The best officers are those who follow the rules and show no favoritism.

Officers supervise inmates at all hours and in all of their activities, from meals to personal-hygiene time. If a conflict occurs, officers must use the least amount of force possible; most officers who directly supervise inmates do not carry firearms, so they must be able to resolve disputes as calmly and peacefully as possible. As a result, excellent listening and communication skills are essential so that officers can understand and direct those in disagreement.

In addition to monitoring inmates, officers are responsible for maintaining the security of the facility both inside and out, and must routinely check all cells, locks, bars, windows, doors, and gates for any sign of tampering or weakness. Both packages and visitors must be inspected and sometimes searched for contraband items such as drugs or weapons. Even inmate mail must be monitored to limit gang activity or the transmission of unlawful information.

The transportation of prisoners is a time of great risk, so officers must be particularly vigilant when inmates are being moved from one facility to another or driven to court dates or medical appointments. As with many law enforcement positions, careful notes or daily logs must be kept of all inmate activity, and reports must be written detailing incidents and violations. Excellent records are essential and must be updated frequently.

> **"Being an officer requires special observational skills. You have to be able to assess the situation and decide quickly how best to proceed so you can avoid a confrontation. Sometimes that requires talking; sometimes you have to postpone a discussion until the prisoner is calmer."**
> —Donald Bosley, Corrections Officer of the Year for 2000, Robert Scott Correctional Facility, Plymoth, Michigan

Keys to Success

To be a successful corrections officer, you should have

- communication and persuasion skills
- teamwork ability
- the capacity to respond quickly to the unexpected
- leadership ability
- physical strength

Do You Have What It Takes?

Students interested in careers as COs should have good judgment and the ability to think on their feet. If you're the kind of person who is emotionally dependable and able to handle difficult situations, corrections work may be for you. While in high school, develop your communication skills through composition and English courses; you will need to be able to communicate clearly and effectively with inmates, coworkers, and your superiors both orally and in written reports. Learn as much as you can about the law and try to achieve positions of responsibility and authority at school, such as those in student government or peer-to-peer counseling groups. The job requires that you be in good health, so it's important to be fit and active. You must also have a clean record, so stay away from unlawful activity.

A Typical Day at Work

Corrections work is scheduled in shifts, which means you should expect to work on nights, weekends, and holidays. Much of your training will take place on the job, so expect to rotate through a variety of duties in your first year. You may be assigned to inspect visitors to make sure they are not carrying in illegal substances such as drugs or alcohol. If you work in the mailroom, you will need to inspect all packages for contraband items such as cash or weapons. One task may be to oversee recreation time in the prison yard, making sure that no fights occur. Perhaps you will be asked to monitor a particular cell block that has been having conflicts between inmates. If so, you will be required to write a report on your observations and formally or informally interview inmates to better understand the nature of the problem so that it can be resolved. Your shift may pass with no incident or may be marked by crises of many kinds, ranging from verbal exchanges with prisoners to physical interventions when necessary.

How to Break In

Most states have a minimum age requirement of 18 to 21 to work in corrections. (COs also must be younger than 35 if they are beginning a career in corrections, unless they've spent time in the military.) While you are waiting to reach the required age, you can acquire an associate's degree in criminal justice or corrections. Courses in human behavior, psychology, and other social sciences will help prepare you to work with the prison population. Work experience will also make you a more attractive candidate, especially if you choose a job in which you are working with people and demonstrating a high degree of responsibility. Volunteer positions are another way to improve your résumé and provide yourself with opportunities to enhance your interpersonal skills. Finally, the military is an excellent place to prepare for a career in corrections.

Two-Year Training

Two-year associate's degree programs in criminal justice or corrections focus on understanding both prison systems and human behavior. Students study psychology, constitutional law, and related courses such as crisis management. With an associate's degree, you'll be better able to meet the challenges of corrections academies, where you will be tested on your understanding of the law as well as the civil rights of inmates, among other topics. In daily work, logs of inmate activity must be kept by each staff member, so writing skills are also important.

All new hires attend training academies for two to four months and then begin their probationary year. On-the-job training teaches officers how to successfully conduct the daily count procedures in which officers on duty carefully account for the inmates. Trainees are also taught emergency response techniques, proper inspection of the facility both for security and sanitation, and the intervention skills.

Should you decide to move forward in your career in corrections, the skills you learn in a two-year program will assist you. What's more, to work in a federal prison, you must have a combination of postsecondary education and/or several years' employment in related fields such as youth counseling, probation work, or security work. Opportunities include advancement to sergeant, lieutenant, and captain, all the way up to warden. Additional education is often required.

What to Look For in a School

When considering a two-year school, be sure to ask these questions:

- Will it prepare me to pass the written portion of the corrections exam in my area?
- Will I learn the skills needed to succeed at the training academy?
- Does the school provide internships or volunteer opportunities at local correctional facilities?
- What are the professors' credentials? Have they worked in corrections and/or at the training academies?
- How available are instructors outside of the classroom?

The Future

Opportunities in corrections will continue to be numerous as the prison population increases. Rigid sentencing laws will keep prison populations high through longer sentences and reduced parole. As a result, new facilities will be built and will require staff. As of 2004, there were 429,000 COs and 38,000 administrators. Both numbers are expected to increase by 6 to 9 percent by 2014, according to the Bureau of Labor Statistics. There is a fairly high turnover in corrections, as officers both advance and leave the field for other jobs. Most states allow officers to retire at age 50 after 20 years of service or at any age with 25 years of service, so positions become available regularly. While promotion is usually based on seniority and job performance, an associate's degree will provide you with knowledge that will aid you while on the job.

Interview with a Professional:
Q &A

Paula Allen

Chief of security, Oregon Department of Corrections,
Salem, Oregon

Q: *How did you get started?*

A: I was taking college classes in the criminal justice program for both law enforcement and corrections. One of the courses included touring local adult and juvenile correctional facilities, where I became aware of the vast opportunities the corrections field had to offer. While still enrolled in school, I had an opportunity to take a temporary job as a correctional officer, and that was nearly seventeen years ago.

Q: *What's a typical day like?*

A: I think most people who work in this field will tell you there isn't a typical day. Every day is filled with new challenges and different problems to solve. Although there's structure to maintain a safe environment for staff, inmates, and the general public, we are in the business of working with people, and along with that comes diversity.

Q: *What's your advice for those starting a career?*

A: It's all about attitude and making the most out of your career. The only limits you have are those that you place upon yourself. In a correctional environment, there are countless avenues you can take in developing a career. In some sense, a prison is like its own city. Within that city, staff provide a variety of services for inmates such as health services, food services, counseling, and trades maintenance just to name a few.

Q: *What's the best part of being a corrections administrator?*

A: There's not just one; it's a combination of things. For example, mentoring new employees and working with others to establish a good working environment. These are all reasons why I love being in this field.

Did You Know?

More than 1 in every 32 American adults—more than 7 million—are on probation or parole, in jail or prison, according to 2005 data from the U.S. Bureau of Justice Statics. State correctional budgets increased 145 percent from 1986 to 2001, according to the bureau.

Job-Seeking Tips

See the suggestions below and turn to Appendix A for advice on résumés and interviews.

✔ Decide what you're interested in and seek relevant experience.

✔ Talk to the career placement office at your school.

✔ Seek out positions of authority and responsibility in your community.

✔ Volunteer in prison literacy programs or similar efforts.

Career Connections

For more information on pursuing a career as a CO, contact the following organizations.

American Jail Association http://www.corrections.com

American Correctional Association http://www.aca.org

Correctional Service Canada http://www.csc-scc.gc.ca

Correction Corporation of America http://www.correctioncorps.com

State Departments of Corrections http://www.corrections.com/andmore/state.html#1

Associate's Degree Programs

Here are a few schools offering quality corrections/criminal justice programs:

Broward Community College, Fort Lauderdale, Florida

Montcalm Community College, Sidney, Michigan

Pierce College, Steilacoom, Washington

Lansing Community College, Lansing, Michigan

Financial Aid

For general information on financial aid for two-year students, turn to Appendix B.

Related Careers

Probation or parole officer, security guard, correctional treatment specialist, and juvenile caseworker.

Forensic Specialist

Vital Statistics

Salary: The median yearly salary for forensic specialists is about $44,000, according to 2006 data from the U.S. Bureau of Labor Statistics.

Employment: Forensics is expected to grow by more than 36 percent over the next seven years (much faster than the average for all occupations through 2014) as improved methods and resources become available through computer-driven technologies, according to the Bureau of Labor Statistics.

Education: A two-year degree in forensics provides instruction in basic science as well as in the more advanced technologies that today's crime scene investigators use.

Work Environment: The work environment is whenever and wherever crimes occur, both inside and outside.

Television shows such as *CSI* and *Law and Order* have introduced the public to the exciting world of forensics, or the investigation of crimes through the use of science and technology. As any viewer knows, we've moved far from the techniques of Sherlock Holmes and the Hardy Boys, both in the fictional world and the real world. Court TV and famous trials, such as that of O.J. Simpson, have elevated the profile of forensic science technicians.

Although technicians who work in laboratories as well as senior crime scene analysts usually have advanced degrees, entry-level positions in crime scene investigation are available to those with two-year degrees in forensics or crime scene technology. These jobs require a love of science and facts as well as the desire to help society. Forensic specialist, CSI (crime scene investigator), ET (evidence technician), CST (crime scene technician), FI (forensic investigator), SOCO (scenes of crime officer), CSA (crime scene analyst), and CO (criminalistics officer) are all used as titles for this line of work.

The goal of everyone who works on the scene of a crime is to uncover the facts in order to solve the crime. This evidence can then be used in the investigation and trial of the suspected criminals involved. Facts are the most compelling part of a case to judges and juries and often convince them of guilt or innocence when witness testimony and circumstantial evidence cannot. As a result, the efforts of crime scene technicians and the people they work with are essential.

Crime scene technicians work with all kinds of physical evidence. This evidence can be invisible to the human eye, such as DNA; visible only with help, such as fingerprints and bodily fluids; or patently obvious, such as the position of corpses or blood-stained vehicles. Crimes scenes are by their very nature disturbing, so this field is only for those who are able to handle working in an often harrowing environment. A crime technician's first job is to secure the scene so that no evidence is compromised. Then, with the help of cameras, fingerprint powder, and other technical aids, technicians must collect, secure, and package all relevant evidence on the scene.

Crime scene technicians also must file detailed reports of what they observe and submit them to the other investigators working on the case. Often technicians participate in meetings and briefings within the law enforcement agency handling the investigation, so their notes and procedure must be impeccable. Teamwork is essential in solving any crime, and team members must do their part to ensure the validity of the evidence. One way to do this is by safeguarding the chain of evidence as it weaves its way from the scene to the technicians to the scientists who test the evidence in the lab. For this reason, those who work on crime scenes must be vigilant and careful people who are well organized and conscientious.

Due to the staffing limitations that smaller police forces face, many crime scene investigators are sworn officers. Greater specialization is possible in larger departments, where civilian crime scene investigators are more common. Because of increasing technological advances within forensics, there is a trend toward more civilian investigators; however, the best opportunities, salaries, and benefits will continue to exist mainly for sworn officers. If you live in a small town or rural area, becoming a sworn officer may be the surest path to advancing to crime scene work.

Whether you decide to enter the field as a civilian or an officer, police and detectives direct investigations and manage evidence as cases are built, so good cooperation and communication skills are essential. Others who are involved include defense lawyers, district attorneys, coroners, and medical examiners. Each person has an important job to do and provides a crucial component in solving crimes. With today's advanced technology, crime scene technicians' jobs are more important than ever in proving the guilt or innocence of the accused, and are an essential element in our judicial system. Very few fields offer the kind of satisfaction that comes from knowing that a criminal is behind bars or an innocent person is cleared because of your efforts.

On the Job

Working on crime scenes is physically and emotionally demanding. Calls come in at any hour, and you must be ready to face what are often terrible circumstances. The work can be dangerous; you are often dealing with the handiwork of violent people who don't want you to catch them. On scene, great care must be taken to keep others from compromising the evidence. Sometimes there is a tremendous amount of evidence to be gathered, and you may work through the night to collect fibers, fingernails, and paint samples or examine footprints, bullet holes, or tire tracks. You must be able to concentrate for hours at a time and work through fatigue to do your job.

As a rookie crime scene technician, you will begin by closely following your superiors to learn proper procedure and technique. Perhaps you will be asked to photograph blood spatter patterns or dig through a victim's garbage to uncover clues. Throughout your training, you must keep meticulous notes so as to better assist your superiors when they write their reports. Often you will accompany them to autopsies where bodies are "processed"—examined for evidence. You may join them at briefings, where you may be relied on for your observations and to collect physical evidence from the body for transport to the lab. In your work, you must be sure to follow very specific protocol for the chain of custody for the evidence so that all data you uncover are legally acceptable in court.

Equipment maintenance is another facet of crime scene work. Cameras must be clean and kits always must be fully stocked for the next emergency. Perhaps you will have to contact the next of kin to inform them of the loss of a loved one. This can be a particularly difficult aspect of the job, one that never gets easier. Similarly, working with corpses also can take its toll, so make sure to build a good support system of friends, family, and peers to lean on should you decide to pursue a career in forensics.

As your strengths become apparent and you advance, you may begin to specialize in a certain area, such as ballistics or fingerprint technology, or you may choose to pursue an advanced degree to increase your opportunities.

> **"This is not just a job, it is a lifelong professional career. It's incredibly rewarding, notwithstanding the toils that are required to play this game. It's fantastic to be able to be the last voice for those who can no longer speak on their own behalf."**
> —Rob Graznow, Director of the Forensic Criminalistics Program, Central Pennsylvania College

Keys to Success

To be a successful forensics specialist, you should have

- concentration and observational skills
- organizational skills

➾ analytical abilities

➾ mechanical aptitude

➾ science, math, and computer skills

➾ tolerance of emotionally challenging scenes

➾ a commitment to justice

A Typical Day at Work

It's 2 a.m. and your cell phone is ringing: it's your fellow crime scene analyst, calling with the address of an apparent murder/suicide. As you throw on some clothes and gather your kit, he tells you that there's been a record of domestic disputes from the address, and it looks like the worst has finally happened.

Driving through the abandoned streets, you brace yourself for what you are about to see. It's never easy to walk into a violent crime scene. You only hope that no children were involved. When you arrive, two police officers are cordoning off the driveway as neighbors stare anxiously from nearby yards.

Your superior officer sends you to the bedroom to dust for fingerprints, examine the sheets for bodily fluids, and scan the room for other clues that might indicate how the crime unfolded. Even though everyone's hunch is that this was a murder/suicide, you still need to be as careful as ever to eliminate any doubt and make sure that a suspect isn't at large. You and your partner divide duties and begin the painstaking process of collecting fibers, hair samples, and any other clues that will close this case.

Three hours later, you emerge from the bedroom with evidence bags carefully secured. You volunteer to drive them to the lab so they can be processed, along with several other items that have been recovered from the house. You leave the scene drained but with the knowledge that you have done your best to help bring this sad case to its conclusion.

Do You Have What It Takes?

Students interested in careers in forensics should love math and science and take as many courses as possible in these two areas. You'll need knowledge of both areas to complete tasks such as calculating bullet trajectories or analyzing gunshot residue. In addition, the job requires good written and oral communication skills. Lab reports and oral presentations often required in science courses are excellent preparation for the responsibilities you'll have in forensic work. Your reports will often provide the basis for an investigation; if they are not clear and well written, the case will suffer. Additional skills such as photography and drawing may be helpful as well. You should also make sure that you can handle the distressing nature of crime scenes. You'll encounter many corpses, so if you pass out when you see blood, crime scene work may not be for you!

How to Break In

Many crime scene investigators begin in law enforcement, so consider volunteering at or even joining your local police force to learn their crime scene procedures as you work toward your associate's degree. You will need to spend several years on the force before you can advance to crime scene work, since it is often a highly sought-after position. If you decide to pursue forensics as a civilian, try to find internship positions that will expose you to the different specialties and opportunities in the field. Occasionally, private employers such as forensic consulting agencies and ballistics experts will help subsidize your training as you work for them. The job requirements of law enforcement agencies and private employers vary, so prepare yourself accordingly by learning the requirements in your area. Remember, there is a difference between training, which is done by the agency employing you, and education, which you receive from a college. The best way to find a position is to be familiar with the requirements and meet them.

Two-Year Training

Two-year associate's degrees in forensics/crime scene investigation provide the foundation that is specifically needed to begin this career and land an entry-level position with a law enforcement agency. Basic courses in mathematics, chemistry, physics, and biology are crucial underpinnings in a profession that depends heavily on scientific methods and knowledge. Lab work is essential and "time on the bench" is hands-on training necessary before you proceed to actual crime scenes. Then you will be better prepared to do your best, where the information you uncover will provide an essential role if the case goes to court.

An associate's degree in forensics will also introduce you to criminal procedure, criminal law, and human psychology. Many programs offer a combination of coursework and apprenticeships in which trainees shadow crime scene investigators. Advanced technologies such as AFIX Tracker and Automated Fingerprint Identification System (AFIS), two fingerprint identification systems, are just a few examples of the new technologies that students will be exposed to in their degree programs. Continuing education is a must in a field that is so dependent on developing technologies. You can also choose to take the International Association for Identification's (IAI) crime scene certification test after one year in crime scene work. The IAI also offers several specialized certifications in areas such as footwear and latent prints. As with any career, advanced training is always an asset that improves your résumé and increases your opportunities within the field.

What to Look For in a School

When considering a two-year school, be sure to ask these questions:

☞ Will this degree program provide both course work and the connections to an apprenticeship?

☞ What is the school's job placement rate?

☞ What areas of specialization does the school offer in terms of careers in forensics?

☞ What are the professors' credentials? Have they worked in the field? How familiar are they with the latest advancements in crime scene technology?

☞ What is the relationship between the school and the local law enforcement agencies?

The Future

As of 2006, according to the Bureau of Labor Statistics, there were 10,000 forensic science technicians, although because that job title is limiting, it may not reflect the total number of people working in the field. Yet statistics show that even within that group, employment is expected to increase by over 36 percent by 2014.

As criminals become more adept in their methods, so do the techniques used to catch them. As a result, the best opportunities will be for graduates who have excellent training in the newest areas of forensics, such as computer-based crime scene reconstruction, and digital photography imaging techniques. Those with greater training will have better chances for advancement, so expect to continue your studies even after you begin work in the field.

Did You Know?

The choice to place the hugely successful original *CSI: Crime Scene Investigation* series in Las Vegas was not random. Among U.S. crime labs, Las Vegas is the second most active, surpassed only by the FBI lab at Quantico, Virginia (imdb.com).

Interview with a Professional:
Q&A
Karie Cain
Deputy coroner, Greenville County Coroner's Office,
Greenville, South Carolina

Q: *How did you get started?*

A: While I was still in school completing my criminal justice degree, I was a deputy coroner through an unpaid internship at the Greenville County Coroner's Office. During this time, I realized this was my calling. I continued to "ride" well after my intern program ended, then became a volunteer, and eventually went full time.

Q: *What's a typical day like?*

A: There is no such thing as a typical day for a deputy coroner. We're on first call-out for seven days, starting at 6 p.m. Sunday and ending 6 p.m. the following Sunday. We respond to all deaths that are unattended. Some deaths are by natural causes, and we simply take information over the phone; others might be homicide, suicide, accidental, or traffics that require us to respond to the scene. If this is the case, we photograph and document the scene, notify next of kin, process the body, and attend the autopsies. We also work directly with law enforcement.

Q: *What's your advice for those starting a career?*

A: My advice is to be very certain that this is the right field for you. Do as much research as you can, and make sure you think it's something you can do every day. Many students come to realize that this isn't the career for them upon attending autopsies and death scenes.

Q: *What's the best part of being a forensic specialist?*

A: The best part of being in the forensic field is the fact that no two crime scenes are the same. I learn something new every day.

Job Seeking Tips

See the suggestions below and turn to Appendix A for advice on résumés and interviews.

✔ Decide which aspects of forensics you're interested in and seek relevant experience.

✔ Talk to the career placement office at your school.

✔ Develop useful skills for the field, such as sketching and photography.

✔ Scan forensics job listings online and learn the requirements in the fields that interest you.

Career Connections

For further information, contact the following organizations.

International Crime Scene Investigators Association http://www.icsia.org

International Association for Identification http://www.theiai.org

American Academy of Forensic Scientists http://www.aafs.org

Canadian Society of Forensic Scientists http://www.csfs.ca

Crime Scene Investigator http://www.crime-scene-investigator.net

Young Forensic Scientists Forum http://www.aafs.org/yfsf/index.htm

Associate's Degree Programs

Here are a few schools offering quality forensics programs:

Anne Arundel Community College, Arnold, Maryland

Griffin Technical College, Griffin, Georgia

Grossmont Community College El Cajon, California

Hudson Valley Community College, Troy, New York

Financial Aid

For information on financial aid for two-year students, turn to Appendix B.

Association of Firearm and Tool Mark Examiners Scholarship http://www.afte.org/AssociationInfo/a_scholarship.htm

Explorer's Scholarship—Federal Criminal Investigators' Service Award (Law Enforcement, $500): The Federal Criminal Investigators Association recognizes Explorers who render outstanding service to law enforcement agencies with a $500 U.S. Savings bond and plaque. http://www.learning-for-life.org/exploring/scholarships/pdf/fia.pdf

Related Careers

Ballistics analyst, computer-related crime investigator, aviation accident investigator, image enhancement specialist, fingerprint analyst, polygraph examiner, and crime scene photographer.

Private Security Specialist

Vital Statistics

Salary: Private detectives earn an average annual income of $32,110 a year; security guards earn between $16,640 and $25,510; and gaming surveillance officers and gaming investigators average $25,840 a year, according to 2006 data from the U.S. Bureau of Labor Statistics.

Employment: The private security field is projected to grow faster than the average for all occupations through 2014, according to the Bureau of Labor Statistics. Opportunities will be ample in a variety of specialized areas, especially those related to computers, intellectual property, and transportation.

Education: A two-year degree in criminal justice or loss prevention will provide instruction in surveillance techniques, security management, and public safety.

Work Environment: The work environment includes offices and private homes, department stores, industrial facilities, and hotels; some work is done from a vehicle.

Today's world has become increasingly concerned with safety. Personal threats such as identity theft and robbery have the potential to affect us all. For those interested in stopping crimes before they happen and finding the people who commit them, a career in security offers many opportunities. Security work focuses on ensuring the safety and well-being not only of people but of their personal information, property, and communities. Work in this field is constantly evolving; as technology develops, both the benefits and threats it creates require those in the field to be flexible and knowledgeable. A two-year degree in programs such as criminal justice, security management, or loss prevention is excellent preparation to meet these demands.

In the world of security, jobs exist both in private industry and the government and entail protecting anything that is considered valuable, from company secrets to a person's identity. Those in security often work with law enforcement officials to prevent crime, enforce laws, and safeguard citizens and property. Security workers are often the true "first responders," on the scene before other emergency personnel have arrived. It is an appealing alternative to those who have considered police work but prefer positions with greater variety and flexibility.

Licensing requirements vary with the position. If the job necessitates carrying a firearm, you will definitely need to have a gun license. Beyond that, rules vary from state to state, as do education requirements. In general, the more reputable and high-profile the firm, the more likely it is that you will have to undergo some kind of licensing process, even if it is not required by your state. Professional organizations and community colleges often offer classes to acquire the necessary certification.

Security workers must also pass rigorous background checks in order to apply for some positions. Many positions require a security clearance, a status granted to individuals whose background has been thoroughly researched. This enables them to handle classified information. Drug screening and psychological testing are also used to eliminate applicants who may be considered risks. Job-seekers with criminal records rarely land positions in security.

Training in the world of security is ongoing, as technology improves and threats change over time. Again, while this training is often voluntary, it is helpful in achieving the best positions. Organizations such as the American Society for Industrial Security International (ASIS) provide guidelines in topics ranging from the use of force to evidence retrieval. Advancement in the field of security is possible if you work hard and develop a résumé that reflects both specialization and competence across a range of security issues.

Security specialists usually begin as employees in larger organizations, but with experience, they often decide to start their own businesses. Security work can supplement a primary income because of the range of opportunities, the flexible scheduling, and the limited training requirements. These factors make competition for jobs more intense. So an associate's degree helps strengthen your chances of finding a quality position. In the more exclusive, competitive, and dangerous positions, salaries are generally higher; so is the level of responsibility.

Security specialists work in a variety of positions, including:

- Personal security
- Loss prevention
- Gaming surveillance
- Site security
- Private investigation
- Legal, corporate, insurance, and financial investigation

On the Job

Those in security often work long, unpredictable hours. They can spend nights, weekends, and holidays trying to break a case or protecting whatever they've been assigned. Your duties may be static, which means that you will be in one location, such as at a post monitoring closed-circuit TV cameras and alarms and noting the comings and goings of familiar and unfamiliar people on site. If you are on mobile patrol, you must know your territory inside out to detect suspicious activities or changes. Walkie-talkies and cellular phones are often used to maintain contact with other patrol forces.

Security work can be dangerous sometimes and may require the use of firearms. Private investigators often catch people in the act of committing crimes or other undesirable behavior. Guards may be expected to apprehend and arrest suspects. Casino security workers often need to escort undesirable guests off the premises. Other positions, such as those in nuclear power plants, include exposure to the significant risks of terrorism, and require specialized training to deal with this threat.

Office work is another aspect of security. Careful records must be kept, documenting incidents and tracking the progress of cases. These records may be used as evidence in court cases, so it is crucial that they be accurate and complete. Security firms or departments often have databases of confidential background information, so security workers must be highly ethical.

Compiling data and conducting interviews are other important elements of security work. Legal, corporate, and financial investigators spend many hours searching through records and talking to people to gain the information to help their case. Computer security specialists spend long hours analyzing and managing networks to keep systems running smoothly and without threats. These specializations often require advanced degrees. If you are interested in these fields, make sure you can transfer credits from your two-year program.

Keys to Success

To be a successful security specialist, you should possess

- patience and persistence
- the ability to remain calm under pressure
- excellent judgment and common sense
- leadership skills
- a clean record
- good social skills
- attention to detail

Do You Have What It Takes?

Students interested in a career as a security specialist need to be excellent communicators, so classes in composition and public speaking will help you write reports and convey information clearly. Your job will often require that you maintain your focus for extended periods, so you should have strong powers of concentration even when faced with monotonous tasks. Depending on your position, you may need to confront people in awkward or dangerous situations, so you should feel comfortable approaching strangers whatever the circumstances.

A Typical Day at Work

Your daily routine will directly depend on what kind of security work you do. For example, you may sit for hours monitoring the activities of a suspect or perhaps a spouse believed to be cheating. Maybe you will tail a claimant in a worker's compensation case to see if his injuries are enough to merit payment. Perhaps you will be part of a team assigned to protect a high-profile family visiting from another country. Regardless, security work takes place at all hours, so you may work night shifts, weekends, and holidays. As an entry-level worker, you may be assigned tasks that require less experience but plenty of attention to detail; be ready to record what you witness or able to clearly communicate essential data and information. Whatever your exact job description may be, your work will require you to be vigilant and conscientious, despite the many hours that may pass without troubling incidents. In fact, if you're doing your job, those are the kinds of days you are trying to achieve.

How to Break In

While working on an associate's degree in protective services, loss prevention, or criminal justice, budding security specialists can gain experience in part-time positions as loss prevention assistants in places such as department stores, hotels, and residential communities. If you are interested in private investigator work, approach local investigators and see if they need help with office work such as filing and correspondence. This will expose you to the field and help you to develop skills you'll need as an investigator. If you are computer-savvy, seek temporary work with companies that provide IT security. Internships with private security firms are another way to develop experience in the field. You can also join professional organizations such as the ASIS International (http://www.asisonline.org) to learn more about the profession. Finally, a résumé that proves that you are dependable and trustworthy will go a long way in an industry that is concerned with safety.

Two-Year Training

Although security is an expanding field, it also attracts a large number of highly qualified candidates. These include retired law enforcement professionals, who, because of early retirement options, are often able to begin second careers when they are still relatively young. A two-year degree in criminal justice, loss prevention, or security management will help to offset a lack of experience in the field. Fortunately, most two-year programs involve time on the job, either as an intern or assistant to someone in the industry. Supplement this time during summer break and holidays.

The skills that you will develop in a two-year training program in security include investigative techniques, firearm handling, and crisis management. Core courses in English composition, computers, and statistics are often part of the curriculum. Depending on your interest, you may decide to focus on white-collar crime and take courses in operating systems like Linux and Windows or study accounting and business. Perhaps you are more drawn to government work, which is as varied as private sector work, although slightly less competitive because of a lower pay scale. If so, visit the appropriate government Web sites for job listings to get a better indication of what kind of training they expect from their applicants. In this way, you can choose programs and courses accordingly and develop a résumé that is tailored to your intended specialty.

Many schools are affiliated with separate training academies that specialize in certain fields, such as loss prevention or private investigation. State and federal programs are also available in certain areas. Your guidance office can lead you to the proper resources to help you find out more about programs offered in your area.

What to Look For in a School

When considering a two-year school, be sure to ask these questions:

☞ Will this degree program provide both course work and the connections to an apprenticeship?

☞ What is the school's job placement rate?

☞ What areas of specialization does the school offer in terms of security?

☞ What are the professors' credentials? Have they worked in the field? How familiar are they with the latest advancements in security?

The Future

Opportunities in the field of security are expanding as budget cuts in state and local law enforcement create a greater dependence on private security firms. Both public and private industries are quickly developing teams to ensure that their personnel, assets, and information are safe and secure. Because of the growing perception of threats, businesses and individuals are hiring security specialists to set up protection systems and monitor the activities not only of outside influences, but also those close to home. Technological advancements raise additional concerns as confidential information becomes more and more vulnerable. The greatest opportunities will exist for those with advanced training in the anticipation, detection, and elimination of the many risks facing our world today.

Interview with a Professional:
Q&A
Rob Constant
Security officer, Roosevelt Hotel, New York, New York

Q: *How did you get started?*

A: I've always been a people person and have enjoyed customer service–related positions that allowed me to help others. I guess it's a calling. Before joining the police academy, I was an auxiliary police officer, and I remain one to this day. That early experience gave me good idea of what I was getting myself into.

Q: *What's a typical day like?*

A: Shifts are either from 7 a.m. to 3 p.m., 3 p.m. to 11 p.m., or 11 p.m. to 7 a.m., but no day is ever the same. One day there might be two or more guests or employees injured or missing property, the next day can go smoothly and quietly without incident. Another day may be spent smiling at guests all day, or, perhaps, throwing an unwanted guest off the property. You just never know.

Q: *What's your advice for those starting a career?*

A: It's helpful if you're a people person because people will look to you for answers. It's also important to have a thick skin in this industry because you'll see and hear everything and anything at any given time. Finally, learn as much about the industry as possible before making your decision. It has many paths, and only you know how far you want to take it.

Q: *What's the best part of being a private security specialist?*

A: The best part is trust. People you've never met will trust you to make the best decision for them. In a time of crisis, sorrow, or happiness, they'll do what you think is best for them, and with the experience gained through training, you'll be able to make that decision on a second's notice. Every day is a trial and every day is a learning experience.

Did You Know?

In June, 1972, Frank Wills, a private security guard working at the Watergate office building, the location of the Democratic National Committee headquarters, uncovered a break-in that triggered a chain of events that exposed the Watergate scandal and eventually led to the resignation of President Richard Nixon.

Job Seeking Tips

See the suggestions below and turn to Appendix A for advice on résumés and interviews.

✔ Decide what you're interested in and seek relevant experience.

✔ Talk to the career placement office at your school.

✔ Demonstrate responsibility by working in positions of authority.

✔ Seek internships or part-time work in the field.

> ## "I like matching wits with criminals, scumbags, and other lowlifes. Occasionally, you actually get to catch one."
> —Leigh Wade, author and former private security specialist

Career Connections

For further information, contact the following organizations.

ASIS International http://www.asisonline.org

Security Management http://www.securitymanagement.com

National Association of Security Companies http://www.nasco.org

Associate's Degree Programs

Here are a few schools offering quality criminal justice or loss prevention programs:

Grossmont College, El Cajon, California

Fox Valley Technical College, Appleton, Wisconsin

Vincennes University, Vincennes, Indiana

Eastern Oklahoma State College, Wilbuton, Oklahoma

Financial Aid

For information on financial aid for two-year students, turn to Appendix B.

Related Careers

Bill and account collector, claim adjuster, appraiser, examiner, and investigator.

Homeland Security Worker

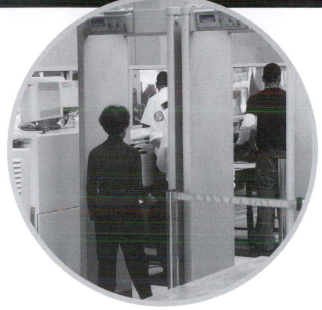

Vital Statistics

Salary: Salaries are as varied as positions, ranging from $25,000 for entry-level positions for border patrol agents to $45,000 for emergency management workers, according to 2006 data from the U.S. Bureau of Labor Statistics.

Employment: Homeland security is a fast-growing field with opportunities increasing between 21 and 35 percent (much more than the average for all occupations) by 2014, according to the Bureau of Labor Statistics.

Education: A two-year degree in homeland security, criminal justice, or emergency management provides a good foundation for a career in this expanding field.

Work Environment: Homeland security work is conducted in offices as well as on individual job sites.

Would you like to help protect our country? Do you enjoy working with others to solve problems and crises? A career in homeland security can provide you with many opportunities to be of service to your country and your neighbors and ensure the safety of both.

Since September 11, concern over our nation's safety has increased tremendously. Threats such as terrorism and biological weapons have become part of our everyday lives, leading to long waits for security checks at airports and metal detectors in the entryway of office buildings, and making us think twice about unattended items on trains and buses. Homeland security workers are responsible for preventing such threats from being realized, reducing our vulnerability to them, responding if an emergency does occur, and minimizing any damage that may result from an attack.

In 2003, the Department of Homeland Security (DHS) was established to manage the national effort to deal with the new challenges facing our country. It currently employs about 183,000 people in 22 different agencies. Canada created its own version of DHS in 2003, and it is known as the Ministry of Public Safety and Emergency Preparedness. The variety of positions in these organizations is as wide as the range of threats we face. Included among these threats are natural disasters such as hurricanes and wildfires as well as technological threats such as computer viruses. With an associate's degree, you can enter the ranks of the homeland security forces in such positions as:

- border patrol agent
- transportation security agent

- emergency management worker
- immigration/customs official
- security specialist

Jobs in homeland security are available in every state in the United States and province in Canada. While most jobs are with federal, state, or local governments, positions are available with private and nonprofit businesses as well. At the state and local level, first responders such as firefighters and police are acting in the interest of homeland security when they are confronted with crises that reach beyond the scope of local incidents. More and more, however, specialized workers are being trained to address the specific threats we perceive as a result of 9/11.

Emergency management can be broken down into four phases: prevention, preparedness, response, and recovery. Each phase involves different tasks. People in emergency management often develop expertise in a particular phase. Yet areas of homeland security work continue to evolve. As our workforces become both more technologically advanced and more interconnected, classified information is vulnerable to greater risks, and steps must be taken to secure it. People who help to ensure that businesses keep running smoothly after disasters are sought by both private and public organizations. A newer field in this sector includes those who safeguard the systems that make our communities function, such as transportation, utility, and public health systems. Professionals in this area try to prevent threats before they occur and also work to minimize damage in the wake of a crisis. Everyone in homeland security works to keep our country running smoothly and tries to ensure minimal disruption to normal life before, during, and after a major emergency.

On the Job

The Department of Homeland Security has a clear and efficient organizational structure with four divisions: Border and Transportation Security; Emergency Preparedness and Response; Chemical, Biological, Radiological and Nuclear Countermeasures; and Information Analysis and Infrastructure Protection. Each division focuses on one aspect of national security.

Border and Transportation Security provides protection for our borders and ports as well as for public and private transportation systems. Nearly 730 million people travel on commercial airlines each year, most with baggage that needs to be screened. There are also 11.2 million trucks and 2.2 million rail cars that enter the United States each year, in addition to 7,500 foreign vessels that enter through U.S. ports. Homeland security workers monitor ports, railways, and airports to ensure that threats are minimized or avoided.

Emergency Preparedness and Response, which used to be known as civil defense, prepares for and responds to any major terrorist strike, natural disaster, or other large-scale emergency. The Federal Emergency Management Agency (FEMA) is in this division. Duties vary by location and depend on the hazards a given area faces. For example, hurricane preparation is of major importance in states like Florida, whereas Kansas must be prepared for tornados. Likewise, major cities such as New York have very different needs compared with smaller towns that face threats to sectors such as agriculture. In the larger cities, jobs are more specialized, while emergency management workers in more rural locations must be able to perform a variety of tasks because of limited budgets and smaller staffs.

It is the responsibility of Chemical, Biological, Radiological and Nuclear Countermeasures to protect our nuclear and chemical plants and prepare for chemical, biological, or nuclear attacks. Information Analysis and Infrastructure Protection monitors the exchange of information among nations, businesses, and individuals to ensure that our country's banks, intelligence operations, and essential services remain unharmed.

Work outside of the Department of Homeland Security includes positions in community service, nonprofit, and educational institutions, in which workers develop emergency plans, educate the community, and conduct research on emergency response, weaknesses in current programs, and contingency plans.

> **"The homeland is secure when the hometown is secure. At the end of the day, America will be as strong as its cities and its regions and its states."**
> —Tom Ridge, U.S. Secretary of Homeland Security, *Lowell Sun*

Keys to Success

To be a successful homeland security worker, you should have

- leadership skills
- a strong desire to help your country
- the ability to respond quickly in a crisis
- good communication skills
- the ability to multitask and prioritize
- a clean record

Do You Have What It Takes?

Students who are interested in homeland security work should enjoy helping people and work well under pressure. Due to the nature of the profession, certain criteria are in place to eliminate risks. These include extensive background checks, security clearances, and psychological and medical evaluations. Beyond these conditions, requirements vary. It's a good idea to visit a few government Web sites to see what specific agencies look for in their potential employees. While you are in high school, courses in psychology, world history, and foreign languages will help you be more sensitive to other cultures in addition to being better able to communicate with those who don't speak English. Volunteer work of any kind is also excellent preparation for a career in homeland security.

A Typical Day at Work

Location is perhaps the most important factor in what makes up a typical day in the field of homeland security. If you are in an urban location, your job will be fairly specific. You may help to develop evacuation plans for government buildings in the event of an emergency. Perhaps you will help to coordinate emergency-response teams, acting as a liaison among fire, police, and emergency medical service (EMS) departments. If you are working for a smaller department in a more rural location, your job will involve a greater variety of duties. If you live in a border state, immigration and customs concerns will top your list of importance. Coastal states such as Florida and California also need to monitor the ports and waterways for violations and threats.

Regardless of where you are located, much of your time will focus on prevention and preparation, which means more predictable schedules, with a blend of office and field work. When an emergency occurs, however, you will be expected to remain on the job for hours at a time, serving those in need.

How to Break In

As with many jobs in security, one of the best ways to break in is to become a volunteer in the area that appeals to you. Organizations such as the Red Cross, the U.S. Citizens Corps, and the Freedom Corps can provide valuable experience and contacts. Military service is another way to break into homeland security work. The Reserve Officer Training Corps (ROTC) program offers training that could enable you to qualify for positions that normally require a bachelor's degree. Depending on your area of interest, you may want to develop your foreign language skills. Spanish is essential if you want to become a border patrol agent, while knowledge of a Middle

Eastern language such as Arabic can make you a compelling applicant in other areas of homeland security.

Two-Year Training

While many schools now offer courses in homeland security, several have begun to offer associate's degrees in the field. These programs concentrate on emergency management, risk assessment, and criminal and forensic investigation. Since so much of a homeland security worker's job may focus on detection of threats and apprehending criminals, an understanding of the principals of law and forensics is essential. As a result, many programs in forensics and criminal justice also offer excellent preparation for careers in homeland security.

Continued education is a must in this field since it is essential to stay informed of new developments. You may consider working toward a certificate in homeland security offered by the American College of Forensics Examiners International (ACFEI). You must have a certain amount of experience in the field before you can qualify and be a member of ACFEI, but working through the five levels of certification is an excellent way to advance your career. Another voluntary certificate is the Certified Emergency Manager, offered by the International Association of Emergency Managers.

What to Look For in a School

When considering a two-year school, be sure to ask these questions:

☞ Will this degree program provide both course work and the connections to an internship?

☞ What is the school's job placement rate?

☞ What are the professors' credentials? Have they worked in the field? How available are the professors outside the classroom?

☞ Can credits from this program be transferred to a four-year college?

The Future

Because homeland security affects all of us, opportunities are widespread and will continue to grow at above-average rates. Many who work in the field often begin in government positions and leave for private sector work after they gain experience. This opens positions for new workers, as does the mandatory retirement age in many DHS positions, such as border patrol. More and more businesses are recognizing the need for trained professionals who can ensure the safety and security of both their personnel and their assets and information in these changing times. Increasingly, homeland security specialists will be relied on to meet these challenges.

Interview with a Professional:
Q &A
Lt. Doug Ross
Upstate homeland security planner, Greenville,
South Carolina

Q: *How did you get started?*

A: In November 2005, I transferred from the South Carolina Law Enforcement Division's arson/bomb section to the homeland security section, where I'm responsible for 14 counties in the upper section of my state. I, along with three other planners, serve all public safety agencies in South Carolina.

Q: *What's a typical day like?*

A: A typical day ensures that the many public safety agencies I am responsible for are up-to-date on current information from the Federal Department of Homeland Security in Washington, D.C. I also make sure that the various local fire, police, and emergency medical services agencies are aware of current financial grant opportunities, grant guidelines, training opportunities, and overall interoperability in the event of a catastrophic or terrorism event in my region. I act as a liaison for agencies that have acquired federal funding through the many grants awarded to South Carolina public safety departments.

Q: *What's your advice for those starting a career?*

A: It's hard work and long hours, but stick with it; I can't think of another job that's more rewarding. Understanding all the complexities about the federal Department of Homeland Security is tedious, but beneficial, as one may desire to transfer departments. When it comes to ensuring the safety of others, the possibilities are endless.

Q: *What's the best part of being a homeland security specialist?*

A: The special pride and camaraderie I feel in being a part of the vast operation of homeland security. What I do on a daily basis has a positive impact on the overall safety of all Americans and that makes me proud.

Job Seeking Tips

See the suggestions below and turn to Appendix A for advice on résumés and interviews.

✔ Decide what phase of homeland security work you're interested in and seek relevant experience.

✔ Talk to the career placement office at your school.

✔ Get certified in first aid and cardiopulmonary resuscitation.

✔ Become a volunteer with the Red Cross or the Citizen Corps.

✔ Seek internships in related fields such as law enforcement or emergency medicine.

Did You Know?

The U.S. government is developing a massive computer system that can collect huge amounts of data and, by linking far-flung information from blogs and e-mail to government records and intelligence reports, search for patterns of terrorist activity. The core of this effort is a little-known system called Analysis, Dissemination, Visualization, Insight, and Semantic Enhancement (ADVISE).

Career Connections

For further information, contact the following organizations.

Department of Homeland Security http://www.dhs.gov

Public Safety and Emergency Preparedness Canada http://www.psepc-sppcc.gc.ca/prg/ns/index-en.asp

National Homeland Security Database http://www.twotigers online.com

Associate's Degree Programs

Here are a few schools offering quality homeland security–related programs:

Monroe Community College, Rochester, New York

Community College of Denver, Denver, Colorado

Fairmont State Community and Technical College, Fairmont, West Virginia

Sonoma College, Petaluma, California

Financial Aid

For general information on financial aid for two-year students, turn to Appendix B.

The **Department of Homeland Security** offers about 300 scholarships and fellowships to undergraduate and graduate students. http://www.dhs.gov/index.shtm.

For information on other federal scholarship opportunities, visit http://www.studentjobs.gov.

Related Careers

Risk assessment analyst, cyber-security specialist, and law enforcement officer.

key points down very well. It should sound natural though, and you should come across as friendly, confident, and assertive. Remember, good eye contact needs to be part of your presentation as well as your everyday approach when meeting prospective employers or leads.

Get Your Résumé Ready

In addition to your elevator speech, another essential job-hunting tool is your résumé. Basically, a résumé is a little snapshot of you in words, reduced to one 8½ x 11-inch sheet of paper (or, at most, two sheets). You need a résumé whether you're in high school, college, or the workforce, and whether you've never held a job or have had many.

At the top of your résumé should be your heading. This is your name, address, phone numbers, and your e-mail address, which can be a sticking point. E-mail addresses such as sillygirl@yahoo.com or drinkingbuddy @hotmail.com won't score you any points. In fact they're a turn-off. So if you dreamed up your address after a night on the town, maybe it's time to upgrade. (Similarly, these days potential employers often check Myspace sites, personal blogs, and Web pages. What's posted there has been known to cost candidates a job offer.)

The first section of your résumé is a concise Job Objective (e.g., "Entry-level agribusiness sales representative seeking a position with a leading dairy cooperative"). These days, with word-processing software, it's easy and smart to adapt your job objective to the position for which you're applying. An alternative way to start a résumé, which some recruiters prefer, is to re-work the Job Objective into a Professional Summary. A Professional Summary doesn't mention the position you're seeking, but instead focuses on your job strengths (e.g., "Entry-level agribusiness sales rep; strengths include background in feed, fertilizer, and related markets and ability to contribute as a member of a sales team"). Which is better? It's your call.

The body of a résumé typically starts with your Job Experience. This is a chronological list of the positions you've held (particularly the ones that will help you land the job you want). Remember: never, never any fudging. However, it is okay to include volunteer positions and internships on the chronological list, as long as they're noted for what they are.

Next comes your Education section. Note: It's acceptable to flip the order of your Education and Job Experience sections if you're still in high school or have gone straight to college and don't have significant work experience. Summarize the major courses in your degree area, any certifications you've achieved, relevant computer knowledge, special seminars, or other school-related experience that will distinguish you. Include your grade average if it's more than 3.0. Don't worry if you haven't finished your degree. Simply write that you're currently enrolled in your program (if you are).

Appendix A
Tools for Career Success

When 20-year-old Justin Schulman started job-hunting for a position as a fitness trainer—his first step toward managing a fitness facility—he didn't mess around. "I immediately opened the Yellow Pages and started calling every number listed under health and fitness, inquiring about available positions," he recalls. Schulman's energy and enterprise paid off: He wound up with interviews that led to several offers of part-time work.

Schulman's experience highlights an essential lesson for jobseekers: There are plenty of opportunities out there, but jobs won't come to you— especially the career-oriented, well-paying ones that that you'll want to stick with over time. You've got to seek them out.

Uncover Your Interests

Whether you're in high school or bringing home a full-time paycheck, the first step toward landing your ideal job is assessing your interests. You need to figure out what makes you tick. After all, there is a far greater chance that you'll enjoy and succeed in a career that taps into your passions, inclinations, and natural abilities. That's what happened with career-changer Scott Rolfe. He was already 26 when he realized he no longer wanted to work in the food industry. "I'm an avid outdoorsman," Rolfe says, "and I have an appreciation for natural resources that many people take for granted." Rolfe turned his passions into his ideal job as a forest technician.

If you have a general idea of what your interests are, you're far ahead of the game. You may know that you're cut out for a health care career, for instance, or one in business. You can use a specific volume of *Top Careers in Two Years* to discover what position to target. If you are unsure of your direction, check out the whole range of volumes to see the scope of jobs available. Ask yourself, what job or jobs would I most like to do if I *already* had the training and skills? Then remind yourself that this is what your two-year training will accomplish.

You can also use interest inventories and skills-assessment programs to further pinpoint your ideal career. Your school or public librarian or guidance counselor should be able to help you locate such assessments. Web sites such as America's Career InfoNet (http://www.acinet.org) and JobWeb (http://www.jobweb.com) also offer interest inventories. Don't forget the help advisers at any two-year college can provide to target your interests. You'll find suggestions for Web sites related to specific careers at the end of each chapter in any *Top Careers in Two Years* volume.

Unlock Your Network

The next stop toward landing the perfect job is networking. The word may make you cringe. But networking isn't about putting on a suit, walking into a roomful of strangers, and pressing your business card on everyone. Networking is simply introducing yourself and exchanging job-related and other information that may prove helpful to one or both of you. That's what Susan Tinker-Muller did. Quite a few years ago, she struck up a conversation with a fellow passenger on her commuter train. Little did she know that the natural interest she expressed in the woman's accounts payable department would lead to news about a job opening there. Tinker-Muller's networking landed her an entry-level position in accounts payable with MTV Networks. She is now the accounts payable administrator.

Tinker-Muller's experience illustrates why networking is so important. Fully 80 percent of openings are *never* advertised, and more than half of all employees land their jobs through networking, according to the U.S. Bureau of Labor Statistics. That's 8 out of 10 jobs that you'll miss if you don't get out there and talk with people. And don't think you can bypass face-to-face conversations by posting your résumé on job sites like Monster.com and Hotjobs.com and then waiting for employers to contact you. That's so mid-1990s! Back then, tens of thousands, if not millions, of job seekers diligently posted their résumés on scores of sites. Then they sat back and waited . . . and waited . . . and waited. You get the idea. Big job sites like Monster and Hotjobs have their place, of course, but relying solely on an Internet job search is about as effective as throwing your résumé into a black hole.

Begin your networking efforts by making a list of people to talk to: teachers, classmates (and their parents), anyone you've worked with, neighbors, worship acquaintances, and anyone you've interned or volunteered with. You can also expand your networking opportunities through the student sections of industry associations (listed at the end of each chapter of *Top Careers in Two Years*); attending or volunteering at industry events, association conferences, career fairs; and through job-shadowing. Keep in mind that only rarely will any of the people on your list be in a position to offer you a job. But whether they know it or not, they probably know someone who knows someone who is. That's why your networking goal is not to ask for a job but the name of someone to talk with. Even when you network with an employer, it's wise to say something like, "You may not

have any positions available, but might you know someone I could talk with to find out more about what it's like to work in this field?"

Also, keep in mind that networking is a two-way street. For instance, you may be talking with someone who has a job opening that isn't appropriate for you. If you can refer someone else to the employer, either person may well be disposed to help you someday in the future.

Dial-Up Help

Call your contacts directly, rather than e-mail them. (E-mails are too easy for busy people to ignore, even if they don't mean to.) Explain that you're a recent graduate in your field; that Mr. Jones referred you; and that you're wondering if you could stop by for 10 or 15 minutes at your contact's convenience to find out a little more about how the industry works. If you leave this message as a voicemail, note that you'll call back in a few days to follow up. If you reach your contact directly, expect that they'll say they're too busy at the moment to see you. Ask, "Would you mind if I check back in a couple of weeks?" Then jot down a note in your date book or set up a reminder in your computer calendar and call back when it's time. (Repeat this above scenario as needed, until you get a meeting.)

Once you have arranged to talk with someone in person, prep yourself. Scour industry publications for insightful articles; having up-to-date knowledge about industry trends shows your networking contacts that you're dedicated and focused. Then pull together questions about specific employers and suggestions that will set you apart from the job-hunting pack in your field. The more specific your questions (for instance, about one type of certification versus another), the more likely your contact will see you as an "insider," worthy of passing along to a potential employer. At the end of any networking meeting, ask for the name of someone else who might be able to help you further target your search.

Get a Lift

When you meet with a contact in person (as well as when you run into someone fleetingly), you need an "elevator speech." This is a summary of up to two minutes that introduces who you are, as well as your experience and goals. An elevator speech should be short enough to be delivered during an elevator ride with a potential employer from the ground level to a high floor. In it, it's helpful to show that 1) you know the business involved; 2) you know the company; 3) you're qualified (give your work and educational information); and 4) you're goal-oriented, dependable, and hardworking. You'll be surprised how much information you can include in two minutes. Practice this speech in front of a mirror until you have the

In addition to these elements, other sections may include professional organizations you belong to and any work-related achievements, awards, or recognition you've received. Also, you can have a section for your interests, such as playing piano or soccer (and include any notable achievements regarding your interests, for instance, placed third in Midwest Regional Piano Competition). You should also note other special abilities, such as "Fluent in French" or "Designed own Web site." These sorts of activities will reflect well on you, whether or not they are job-related.

You can either include your references or simply note, "References upon Request." Be sure to ask your references permission to use their name and alert them to the fact that they may be contacted, before you include them on your résumé. For more information on résumé writing, check out Web sites such as http://www.resume.monster.com.

Craft Your Cover Letter

When you apply for a job either online or by mail, it's appropriate to include a cover letter. A cover letter lets you convey extra information about yourself that doesn't fit or isn't always appropriate in your résumé. For instance, in a cover letter, you can and should mention the name of anyone who referred you to the job. You can go into some detail about the reason you're a great match, given the job description. You also can address any questions that might be raised in the potential employer's mind (for instance, a gap in your résumé). Don't, however, ramble on. Your cover letter should stay focused on your goal: to offer a strong, positive impression of yourself and persuade the hiring manager that you're worth an interview. Your cover letter gives you a chance to stand out from the other applicants and sell yourself. In fact, 23 percent of hiring managers say a candidate's ability to relate his or her experience to the job at hand is a top hiring consideration, according to a Careerbuilder.com survey.

You can write a positive, yet concise cover letter in three paragraphs: An introduction containing the specifics of the job you're applying for; a summary of why you're a good fit for the position and what you can do for the company; and a closing with a request for an interview, contact information, and thanks. Remember to vary the structure and tone of your cover letter. For instance, don't begin every sentence with "I."

Ace Your Interview

Preparation is the key to acing any job interview. This starts with researching the company or organization you're interviewing with. Start with the firm, group, or agency's own Web site. Explore it thoroughly; read about their products and services, their history, and sales and marketing information.

Check out their news releases, links that they provide, and read up on or Google members of the management team to get an idea of what they may be looking for in their employees.

Sites such as http://www.hoovers.com enable you to research companies across many industries. Trade publications in any industry (such as *Food Industry News, Hotel Business,* and *Hospitality Technology*) are also available online or in hard copy at many college or public libraries. Don't forget to make a phone call to contacts you have in the organization to get an even better idea of the company culture.

Preparation goes beyond research, however. It includes practicing answers to common interview questions:

☞ *Tell me about yourself* (Don't talk about your favorite bands or your personal history; give a brief summary of your background and interest in the particular job area.)

☞ *Why do you want to work here?* (Here's where your research into the company comes into play; talk about the firm's strengths and products or services.)

☞ *Why should we hire you?* (Now is your chance to sell yourself as a dependable, trustworthy, effective employee.)

☞ *Why did you leave your last job?* (This is not a talk show. Keep your answer short; never bad-mouth a previous employer. You can always say something simply such as, "It wasn't a good fit, and I was ready for other opportunities.")

Rehearse your answers, but don't try to memorize them. Responses that are natural and spontaneous come across better. Trying to memorize exactly what you want to say is likely to both trip you up and make you sound robotic.

As for the actual interview, to break the ice, offer a few pleasant remarks about the day, a photo in the interviewer's office, or something else similar. Then, once the interview gets going, listen closely and answer the questions you're asked, versus making any other point that you want to convey. If you're unsure whether your answer was adequate, simply ask, "Did that answer the question?" Show respect, good energy, and enthusiasm, and be upbeat. Employers are looking for people who are enjoyable to be around, as well as good workers. Show that you have a positive attitude and can get along well with others by not bragging during the interview, overstating your experience, or giving the appearance of being too self-absorbed. Avoid one-word answers, but at the same time don't blather. If you're faced with a silence after giving your response, pause for a few seconds, and then ask, "Is there anything else you'd like me to add?" Never look at your watch or answer your cellphone during an interview.

Near the interview's end, the interviewer is likely to ask you if you have any questions. Make sure that you have a few prepared, for instance:

☞ *"Tell me about the production process."*

☞ *"What's your biggest short-term challenge?"*

☞ *"How have recent business trends affected the company?"*

☞ *"Is there anything else that I can provide you with to help you make your decision?"*

☞ *"When will you make your hiring decision?"*

During a first interview, never ask questions like, "What's the pay?" "What are the benefits?" or "How much vacation time will I get?"

Find the Right Look

Appropriate dressing and grooming is also essential to interviewing success. For business jobs and many other occupations, it's appropriate to come to an interview in a nice (not stuffy) suit. However, different fields have various dress codes. In the music business, for instance, "business casual" reigns for many jobs. This is a slightly modified look, where slacks and a jacket are just fine for a guy, and a nice skirt and blouse and jacket or sweater are acceptable for a woman. Dressing overly "cool" will usually backfire.

In general, watch all of the basics from the shoes on up (no sneakers or sandals, and no overly high heels or short skirts for women). Also avoid attention-getting necklines, girls. Keep jewelry and other "bling" to a minimum. Tattoos and body jewelry are becoming more acceptable, but if you can take out piercings (other than in your ear), you're better off. Similarly, unusual hairstyles or colors may bias an employer against you, rightly or wrongly. Make sure your hair is neat and acceptable (get a haircut?). Also go light on the makeup, self-tanning products, body scents, and other grooming agents. Don't wear a baseball cap or any other type of hat; and by all means, take off your sunglasses!

Beyond your physical appearance, you already know to be well bathed to minimize odor (leave your home early if you tend to sweat, so you can cool off in private), make good eye contact, smile, speak clearly using proper English, use good posture (don't slouch), offer a firm handshake, and arrive within five minutes of your interview. (If you're unsure of where you're going, "Mapquest" it and consider making a dry-run to the site so you won't be late.) First impressions can make or break your interview.

Remember Follow-Up

After your interview, send a thank you note. This thoughtful gesture will separate you from most of the other candidates. It demonstrates your ability to follow through, and it catches your prospective employer's attention one more time. In a 2005 Careerbuilder.com survey, nearly 15 percent of 650 hiring managers said they wouldn't hire someone who failed to send a thank you letter after the interview. Thirty-two percent say they would still consider the candidate, but would think less of him or her.

So do you hand write or e-mail the thank you letter? The fact is that format preferences vary. One in four hiring managers prefer to receive a thank you note in e-mail form only; 19 percent want the e-mail, followed up with a hard copy; 21 percent want a typed hard-copy only; and 23 percent prefer just a handwritten note. (Try to check with an assistant on the format your potential employer prefers.) Otherwise, sending an e-mail and a handwritten copy is a safe way to proceed.

Winning an Offer

There are no sweeter words to a job hunter than "We'd like to hire you." So naturally, when you hear them, you may be tempted to jump at the offer. *Don't.* Once an employer wants you, he or she will usually give you some time to make your decision and get any questions you may have answered. Now is the time to get specific about salary and benefits, and negotiate some of these points. If you haven't already done so, check out salary ranges for your position and area of the country on sites such as Payscale.com, Salary.com, and Salaryexpert.com (basic info is free; specific requests are not). Also, find out what sorts of benefits similar jobs offer. Then don't be afraid to negotiate in a diplomatic way. Asking for better terms is reasonable and expected. You may worry that asking the employer to bump up his offer may jeopardize your job, but handled intelligently, negotiating for yourself in fact may be a way to impress your future employer—and get a better deal for yourself.

After you've done all the hard work that successful job-hunting requires, you may be tempted to put your initiative into autodrive. However, the efforts you made to land your job-from clear communication to enthusiasm-are necessary now to pave your way to continued success. As Danielle Little, a human-resources assistant, says, "You must be enthusiastic and take the initiative. There is an urgency to prove yourself and show that you are capable of performing any and all related tasks. If your manager notices that you have potential, you will be given additional responsibilities, which will help advance your career." So do your best work on the job, and build your credibility. Your payoff will be career advancement and increased earnings.

Appendix B
Financial Aid

One major advantage of earning a two-year degree is that it is much less expensive than paying for a four-year school. Two years is naturally going to cost less than four, and two-year graduates enter the workplace and start earning a paycheck sooner than their four-year counterparts.

The latest statistics from the College Board show that average yearly total tuition and fees at a public two-year college is $2,191, compared to $5,491 at a four-year public college. That cost leaps to more than $21,000 on average for a year at a private four-year school.

With college costs relatively low, some two-year students overlook the idea of applying for financial aid at all. But the fact is, college dollars are available whether you're going to a trade school, community college, or university. About a third of all Pell Grants go to two-year public school students, and while two-year students receive a much smaller percentage of other aid programs, the funding is there for many who apply.

How Does Aid Work?

Financial aid comes in two basic forms: merit-based and need-based.

Merit-based awards are typically funds that recognize a particular talent or quality you may have, and they are given by private organizations, colleges, and the government. Merit-based awards range from scholarships for good writing to prizes for those who have shown promise in engineering. There are thousands of scholarships available for students who shine in academics, music, art, science, and more. Resources on how to get these awards are provided later in this chapter.

Need-based awards are given according to your ability to pay for college. In general, students from families that have less income and fewer assets receive more financial aid. To decide how much of this aid you qualify for, schools look at your family's income, assets, and other information regarding your finances. You provide this information on a financial aid form—usually the federal government's Free Application for Federal Student Aid (FAFSA). Based on the financial details you provide, the school of your choice calculates your Expected Family Contribution (EFC). This is the amount you are expected to pay toward your education each year.

Once your EFC is determined, a school uses this simple formula to figure out your financial aid package:

Cost of attendance at the school

   – **Your EFC**

   – **Other outside aid (private scholarships)**

   = **Need**

Schools put together aid packages that meet that need using loans, work-study, and grants.

Know Your School

When applying to a school, it's a good idea to find out their financial aid policy and history. Read over the school literature or contact the financial aid office and find out the following:

✔ *Is the school accredited?* Schools that are not accredited usually do not offer as much financial aid and are not eligible for federal programs.

✔ *What is the average financial aid package at the school?* The typical award size may influence your decision to apply or not.

✔ *What are all the types of assistance available?* Check if the school offers federal, state, private, or institutional aid.

✔ *What is the school's loan default rate?* The default rate is the percentage of students who took out federal student loans and failed to repay them on time. Schools that have a high default rate are often not allowed to offer certain federal aid programs.

✔ *What are the procedures and deadlines for submitting financial aid?* Policies can differ from school to school.

✔ *What is the school's definition of satisfactory academic progress?* To receive financial aid, you have to maintain your academic performance. A school may specify that you keep up at least a C+ or B average to keep getting funding.

✔ *What is the school's job placement rate?* The job placement rate is the percentage of students who find work in their field of study after graduating.

You'll want a school with a good placement rate so you can earn a good salary that may help you pay back any student loans you have.

Be In It to Win It

The key to getting the most financial aid possible is filling out the forms, and you have nothing to lose by applying. Most schools require that you file the FAFSA, which is *free* to submit, and you can even do it online. For more information on the FAFSA, visit the Web site at http://www.fafsa.ed.gov. If you have any trouble with the form, you can call 1-800-4-FED-AID for help.

To receive aid using the FAFSA, you must submit the form soon after January 1 prior to the start of your school year. A lot of financial aid is delivered on a first-come, first-served basis, so be sure to apply on time.

Filing for aid will require some work to gather your financial information. You'll need details regarding your assets and from your income tax forms, which include the value of all your bank accounts and investments. The form also asks if you have other siblings in college, the age of your parents, or if you have children. These factors can determine how much aid you receive.

Three to four weeks after you submit the FAFSA, you receive a document called the Student Aid Report (SAR). The SAR lists all the information you provided in the FAFSA and tells you how much you'll be expected to contribute toward school, or your Expected Family Contribution (EFC). It's important to review the information on the SAR carefully and make any corrections right away. If there are errors on this document, it can affect how much financial aid you'll receive.

The Financial Aid Package

Using information on your SAR, the school of your choice calculates your need (as described earlier) and puts together a financial aid package. Aid packages are often built with a combination of loans, grants, and work-study. You may also have won private scholarships that will help reduce your costs.

Keep in mind that aid awarded in the form of loans has to be paid back with interest just like a car loan. If you don't pay back according to agreed upon terms, you can go into *default*. Default usually occurs if you've missed payments for 180 days. Defaulted loans are often sent to collection agencies, which can charge costly fees and even take money owed out of your wages. Even worse, a defaulted loan is a strike on your credit history. If you have a negative credit history, lenders may deny you a mortgage, car loan, or other personal loan. There's also financial incentive for paying back on time— many lenders will give a 1 percent discount or more for students who make consecutive timely payments. The key is not to borrow more than you can afford. Know exactly how much your monthly payments will be on a loan when it comes due and estimate if those monthly payments will fit in your future budget. If you ever do run into trouble with loan payments, don't hesitate to contact your lender and see if you can come up with a new payment arrangement—lenders want to help you pay rather than see you go into default. If you have more than one loan, look into loan consolidation, which can lower overall monthly payments and sometimes lock in interest rates that are relatively low.

The Four Major Sources of Aid

U.S. Government Financial Aid

The federal government is the biggest source of financial aid. To find all about federal aid programs, visit http://www.studentaid.fed.gov or call 1-800-4-FED-AID with any questions. Download the free brochure *Funding Education Beyond High School*, which tells you all the details on federal programs. To get aid from federal programs you must be a regular student working toward a degree or certificate in an eligible program. You also have to have a high school diploma or equivalent, be a U.S. citizen or eligible noncitizen and have a valid Social Security number (check http://www.ssa.gov for info). If you are a male aged 18–25, you have to register for the Selective Service. (Find out more about that requirement at http://www.sss.gov or call 1-847-688-6888.) You must also certify that you are not in default on a student loan and that you will use your federal aid only for educational purposes.

Some specifics concerning federal aid programs can change a little each year, but the major programs are listed here and the fundamentals stay the same from year to year. (Note that amounts you receive generally depend on your enrollment status—whether it be full-time or part-time.)

Pell Grant

For students demonstrating significant need, this award has been ranging between $400 and $4,050. The size of a Pell grant does not depend on how much other aid you receive.

Supplemental Educational Opportunity Grant (SEOG)

Again for students with significant need, this award ranges from $100 to $4,000 a year. The size of the SEOG can be reduced according to how much other aid you receive.

Work-Study

The Federal Work-Study Program provides jobs for students showing financial need. The program encourages community service and work related to a student's course of study. You earn at least minimum wage and are paid at least once a month. Again, funds must be used for educational expenses.

Perkins Loans

With a low interest rate of 5 percent, this program lets students who can document the need borrow up to $4,000 a year.

Stafford Loans

These loans are available to all students regardless of need. However, students with need receive *subsidized* Staffords, which do not accrue interest while you're in school or in deferment. Students without need can take *unsubsidized* Staffords, which do accrue interest while you are in school or in deferment. Interest rates vary but can go no higher than 8.25 percent. Loan amounts vary too, according to what year of study you're in and whether you are financially dependent on your parents or not. Students defined as independent of their parents can borrow much more. (Students who have their own kids are also defined as independent. Check the exact qualifications for independent and dependent status on the federal government Web site http://www.studentaid.fed.gov.)

PLUS Loans

These loans for parents of dependent students are also available regardless of need. Parents with good credit can borrow up to the cost of attendance minus any other aid received. Interest rates are variable but can go no higher than 9 percent.

Tax Credits

Depending on your family income, qualified students can take federal tax deductions for education with maximums ranging from $1,500 to $2,000.

AmeriCorps

This program provides full-time educational awards in return for community service work. You can work before, during, or after your postsecondary education and use the funds either to pay current educational expenses or to repay federal student loans. Americorps participants work assisting teachers in Head Start, helping on conservation projects, building houses for the homeless, and doing other good works. For more information, visit http://www.AmeriCorps.gov

State Financial Aid

All states offer financial aid, both merit-based and need-based. Most states use the FAFSA to determine eligibility, but you'll have to contact your state's higher education agency to find out the exact requirements. You can get contact information for your state at http://www.bcol02.ed.gov/Programs/EROD/org_list.cfm. Most of the state aid programs are available only if you study at a school in the state where you reside. Some states are very generous, especially if you're attending a state college or university. California's Cal Grant program gives needy state residents free tuition at in-state public universities.

School-Sponsored Financial Aid

The school you attend may offer its own loans, grants, and work programs. Many have academic- or talent-based scholarships for top-performing students. Some two-year programs offer cooperative education opportunities where you combine classroom study with off-campus work related to your major. The work gives you hands-on experience and some income, ranging from $2,500 to $15,000 per year depending on the program. Communicate with your school's financial aid department and make sure you're applying for the most aid you can possibly get.

Private Scholarships

While scholarships for students heading to four-year schools may be more plentiful, there are awards for the two-year students. Scholarships reward students for all sorts of talent—academic, artistic, athletic, technical, scientific, and more. You have to invest time hunting for the awards that you might qualify for. The Internet now offers many great scholarship search services. Some of the best ones are:

> The College Board (http://www.collegeboard.com/pay)
>
> FastWeb! (http://www.fastweb.monster.com)
>
> MACH25 (http://www.collegenet.com)
>
> Scholarship Research Network (http://www.srnexpress.com)
>
> SallieMae's College Answer (http://www.collegeanswer.com)

Note: Be careful of scholarship-scam services that charge a fee for finding you awards but end up giving you nothing more than a few leads that you could have gotten for free with a little research on your own. Check out the Federal Trade Commission's Project ScholarScam (http://www.ftc.gov/bcp/conline/edcams/scholarship).

In your hunt for scholarship dollars, be sure to look into local community organizations (the Elks Club, Lions Club, PTA, etc.), local corporations, employers (your employer or your parents' may offer tuition assistance), trade groups, professional associations (National Electrical Contractors Association, etc.), clubs (Boy Scouts, Girl Scouts, Distributive Education Club of America, etc.), heritage organizations (Italian, Japanese,

Chinese, and other groups related to ethnic origin), church groups, and minority assistance programs.

Once you find awards you qualify for, you have to put in the time applying. This usually means filling out an application, writing a personal statement, and gathering recommendations.

General Scholarships

A few general scholarships for students earning two-year degrees are

Coca-Cola Scholars Foundation, Inc.

Coca-Cola offers 350 thousand-dollar scholarships (http://www.coca colascholars.org) per year specifically for students attending two-year institutions.

Phi Theta Kappa (PTK)

This organization is the International Honor Society of the Two-Year College. PTK is one of the sponsors of the All-USA Academic Team program, which annually recognizes 60 outstanding two-year college students (http://scholarships.ptk.org). First, Second, and Third Teams, each consisting of 20 members, are selected. The 20 First Team members receive stipends of $2,500 each. All 60 members of the All-USA Academic Team and their colleges receive extensive national recognition through coverage in *USA TODAY*. There are other great scholarships for two-year students listed on this Web site.

Hispanic Scholarship Fund (HSF)

HSF's High School Scholarship Program (http://www.hsf.net/scholar ship/programs/hs.php) is designed to assist high school students of Hispanic heritage obtain a college degree. It is available to graduating high school seniors who plan to enroll full-time at a community college during the upcoming academic year. Award amounts range from $1,000 to $2,500.

The Military

All branches of the military offer tuition dollars in exchange for military service. You have to decide if military service is for you. The Web site http://www.myfuture.com attempts to answer any questions you might have about military service.

Lower Your Costs

In addition to getting financial aid, you can reduce college expenses by being a money-smart student. Here are some tips.

Use Your Campus

Schools offer perks that some students never take advantage of. Use the gym. Take in a school-supported concert or movie night. Attend meetings and lectures with free refreshments.

Flash Your Student ID

Students often get discounts at movies, museums, restaurants, and stores. Always be sure to ask if there is a lower price for students and carry your student ID with you at all times. You can often save 10 to 20 percent on purchases.

Budget Your Funds

Writing a budget of your income and expenses can help you be a smart spender. Track what you buy on a budget chart. This awareness will save you dollars.

Share Rides

Commuting to school or traveling back to your hometown? Check and post on student bulletin boards for ride shares.

Buy Used Books

Used textbooks can cost half as much as new. Check your campus bookstore for deals and also try http://www.eCampus.com and http://www.bookcentral.com

Put Your Credit Card in the Freezer

That's what one student did to stop overspending. You can lock your card away any way you like, just try living without the ease of credit for awhile. You'll be surprised at the savings.

A Two-Year Student's Financial Aid Package

Minnesota State Colleges and Universities provides this example of how a two-year student pays for college. Note how financial aid reduces his out-of-pocket cost to about $7,000 per year.

Jeremy's Costs for One Year

Jeremy is a freshman at a two-year college in the Minnesota. He has a sister in college, and his parents own a home but have no other significant savings. His family's income: $42,000.

College Costs for One Year

Tuition	$3,437
Fees	$388
Estimated room and board*	$7,200
Estimated living expenses**	$6,116
Total cost of attendance	*$17,141*

Jeremy's Financial Aid

Federal grants (does not require repayment)	$2,800
Minnesota grant (does not require repayment)	$676
Work-study earnings	$4,000
Student loan (requires repayment)	$2,625
Total financial aid	*$10,101*

Total cost to Jeremy's family | *$7,040*

* Estimated cost reflecting apartment rent rate and food costs. The estimates are used to calculate the financial aid. If a student lives at home with his or her parents, the actual cost could be much less, although the financial aid amounts may remain the same.

** This is an estimate of expenses including transportation, books, clothing, and social activities.

Index